Dear Tim,

Merry Christmas!

May The Baseball Gods always be with you!

Namaste,

Jonathan
Fink

THE BASEBALL GODS ARE REAL VOLUME 3

The

BASEBALL GODS *are* REAL

Vol. 3: THE RELIGION *of* BASEBALL

JONATHAN A. FINK

The Baseball Gods are Real: Volume 3 – The Religion of Baseball

Written by Jonathan A. Fink
Copyright 2021

Polo Grounds Publishing LLC

Credit and thank you to Meg Reid for book cover design and book layout.

Credit and thank you to Meg Schader for editing.

Credit and thank you to Leon Macapagal for book cover photo.

Credit and thank you to Kim Watson for Jonathan Fink's biography photo-graph.

Credit and thank you to Abi Laksono for Polo Grounds Publishing logo.

A special thank you to my parents Beth and Jeffrey Fink.

This book is dedicated to Tyler Skaggs, The Los Angeles Angel

TABLE OF CONTENTS

THE INTRODUCTION

THE FIRST BOOK I AUTHORED, THE BASEBALL GODS ARE
Real: A True Story About Baseball and Spirituality, was
autobiographical and chronicled the first 42 years of my life.
I discussed my love of baseball and many of the important
events in my life, including a midlife crisis at the age of 38
which inspired me to explore a spiritual path. A few chapters
in the book revealed how I transformed myself through the
practice of yoga and meditation. At about the same time, I was
introduced to one of the mysterious forces in the universe, the
work of the Baseball Gods.

In my second book, *The Baseball Gods are Real - Volume
2: The Road to the Show*, I continued on my spiritual journey and chronicled the next chapters of my life. After 13
years as a financial advisor with Morgan Stanley, I started my
own socially responsible investment firm, Satya Investment
Management. Thereafter I had a chance encounter with
professional baseball player Jon Perrin who was working at

a restaurant at that time, an off-season job. A blossoming friendship led to his apprenticeship with me, which eventually led him to join my firm as a professionally licensed investment advisor. This second book also chronicled Perrin's own journey through baseball's minor league system, from his early days climbing the ranks in the Milwaukee Brewers organization to his eventual trade to the Kansas City Royals.

In this book, my third in the series, The *Baseball Gods are Real - Volume 3: The Religion of Baseball*, I pay homage to the Baseball Gods and set out to praise all things related to baseball and spirituality. The book focuses on what many describe as baseball miracles, celebrates baseball's cathedrals, applauds baseball's saints and calls out its sinners. The book also acknowledges the baseball fanatics, whom I affectionally refer to as the zealots, and magnifies many of the rituals and superstitions that help make baseball the wonderful, mysterious, enjoyable game it is.

Finally, this book explores baseball karma, examines freak injuries, and searches for the fingerprints of the Baseball Gods from beginning to end. It celebrates Baseball Gods moments and even explores the paranormal world of baseball, including baseball tales of ghosts and, believe it or not, UFOs. Rounding third base and heading for home, this book looks ahead to the golden age of baseball yet to come.

As I am sure you can tell from this introduction alone, I am passionate about baseball and have been ever since my first catch with my dad in the backyard of our home on Long Island in Merrick, New York. I hope you enjoy reading this book as much as I enjoyed writing it. May the Baseball Gods always be with you!

CHAPTER ONE

The Religiosity of Baseball

"Religion is belief in someone else's experience. Spirituality is
having your own experience."
—Deepak Chopra

LET ME START BY SAYING THERE ARE A NUMBER OF
interesting similarities between baseball and organized religion. Baseball stadiums are beautiful and individually unique
as are churches, synagogues, temples and mosques. The game
of baseball is filled with ceremony, tradition, ritual, numerology and superstition just like many religions in the world.
Many who closely follow baseball worship the sport, make
sacrifices, pray for their team and suffer when their team
loses. These emotions are also common in religion. Baseball
and organized religion both offer a sense of community, hope,
faith and their followers even believe in miracles.

Writers, poets and authors in years past have tried to
capture the spirit of baseball in a religious context. In his 1919
essay "Baseball as a National Religion," Harvard educated
philosopher and legal scholar Morris R. Cohen said that

baseball provided the essence of religious experience because fans unite in a "mystic unity with a larger life of which we are a part." More recently, sports historian John Thorn, author of *Baseball in the Garden of Eden*, described baseball as not just a religion, but rather as a sectarian national religion. Lawyer and academic John Sexton, author of *Baseball as a Road to God*, conveyed that the game of baseball had that "special something" that gave it some of the qualities that we typically associate with religion. In an interview with "Religion and Ethics Newsweekly" in 2013, Sexton, who also served as the Dean of the New York University School of Law and thereafter as the fifteenth President of the university, said, "Baseball is an avenue to that in the sense that there is this dimension that we experience in baseball of that which can't be put into words...In baseball, as in religion, the seemingly impossible is part of the game." Gary Laderman, Professor of American Religious History and Cultures at Emory University, pointed out that the game of baseball does not need the Baseball Gods or even the holy spirit to be a religious phenomenon. In his *Huffington Post* article named "Is Baseball Sacred?" Laderman noted that, "What truly makes baseball a potentially religious phenomenon is not the presence of God, but that on a more basic level it can be sacred.

I am certain that Morris Cohen, John Thorn, John Sexton and Gary Laderman would agree with me that the game of baseball is not just religious, but also spiritual. In fact, the game's religious and spiritual foundation can be traced back to the prehistories of baseball.

CHAPTER TWO

The Prehistories of Baseball

"The one constant through all the years, Ray, has been baseball. America has rolled by like an army of steamrollers. Is has been erased like a blackboard, rebuilt and erased again. But baseball has marked the time. This field, this game: it's part of our past, Ray. It reminds us of all that was once good and could be again."
— Terence Mann, from the movie *Field of Dreams*

LONG BEFORE MY DAD, JEFFREY FINK, AND MY UNCLE Eddie Fink learned to play alternative versions of baseball such as "stickball," "punchball" and "stoopball" growing up on the concrete streets of the Bronx in New York City, the game of baseball was played in many different forms over hundreds of years, going back to medieval times in ancient Europe. The folk games that most closely resemble modern-day baseball started in the British Islands, but the religious and spiritual foundations for the game were arguably established long before that in ancient Ireland.

In his book *The Prehistories of Baseball*, Seelochan Beharry uncovered that it was the Celts, the people of ancient Ireland, who perhaps most deserve credit for establishing the origins of the game of baseball. Beharry discovered that the roots of baseball originated from primal modes of warfare, such as heaving rocks from a distance at an enemy became throwing, close quarters combat with sticks became hitting, and the wartime strategy of attack and retreat became running. His research revealed that the Celts made sacrifices to three gods, reminiscent of the modern game's rules of three strikes and you're out and three outs and the inning is over. The ancient Celts made sacrifices on three different altars that were set up in a clearing resembling today's modern-day baseball diamond featuring three bases. The Celts also buried their dead underground, as is done today in America and elsewhere, but after filling the grave with dirt, more dirt was placed on top to form what is known as a "burial mound." Burial mounds were considered sacred and no one walked on them out of respect. Members of the community would regularly gather and meet near this higher ground, similar to the way baseball players today gather around the pitcher's mound at a crucial point in a ballgame.

Moving forward from its ancestral past, what would eventually become the modern game of baseball in America as we know it today took shape in the 1500s in England. First, the folk game "rounders" became popular. Rounders, which has many similarities to baseball, now has an official governing body in Ireland and is still played today in the United Kingdom. At about the same time, the game of "stoolball" became a big hit. Also possessing similarities to baseball, stoolball is considered the ancestor of cricket and is sometimes described as "cricket in the air." Lastly, the game of "cricket" became enormously popular throughout the United Kingdom and its territories and remains so still today. As European immigrants travelled to America in the 1700s and 1800s seeking religious freedom and economic opportunity, they brought with them their hopes, aspirations and culture, including their favorite ball games.

These new immigrants came to America with skills that were passed down to them by their fathers and grandfathers. Some were city planners, some were architects, and some were builders. Researching this subject, I learned that many of our nation's founding fathers, including those with the knowledge of building and construction, belonged to secret societies which date back to 14th century Europe. Members in these fraternal organizations passed down their building design knowledge and experience from mentor to apprentice, from generation to generation. Other members passed down sacred secrets and revered knowledge of geometry and numerology.

Almost all numerology in the game of baseball can be traced back to the number three, an important number to the ancient Celts. Perhaps it is not a coincidence that there are three strikes for an out, three outs in an inning, nine field positions, nine innings in a game, and twenty-seven outs per game. I believe the knowledge and experience those new immigrant architects brought here to America may have, in some way, helped future generations to build our nation's first baseball stadiums. I fondly refer to these stadiums as —The Cathedrals.

CHAPTER THREE

The Cathedrals

"These old ballparks are like cathedrals in America. We don't have
big old Gothic cathedrals like they do in Europe.
But we got baseball parks."
—Jimmy Buffett

HAVE YOU EVER NOTICED THAT ALMOST EVERY SPORT IN
America is played on a rectangular field except baseball?
Football, basketball, tennis, pickleball, soccer, volleyball,
badminton, and racquetball all have rectangular playing
surfaces. These sports also have another feature in common.
The metrics of their respective playing areas are exactly the
same everywhere that particular game is played. For example, in tennis, whether the match is played at the Australian
Open, the U.S. Open, the French Open or even at Wimbledon,
the playing surface is always exactly the same size. This is the
case even if the surface is clay at Roland-Garros in Paris, grass
at Wimbledon in the suburbs of London, or on pavement in
the borough of Queens in New York City. But in the game of
baseball, this is not the case, and probably never will be.

Some aspects of every professional baseball field are exactly same. For example, there are four bases, first base, second base, third base and home plate, and they are always ninety feet apart. And the distance between the pitcher's mound and home plate is always 60 feet, 6 inches. Also, all baseball stadiums have foul polls down the left and right field lines. However, that is where the similarities end. All across the country, from Fenway Park in Boston to Miller Park in Milwaukee to Dodger Stadium in Los Angeles, almost every ballpark has its own unique personality and most have different outfield dimensions. Just like every church in my home town of Kansas City and the surrounding suburban area, every baseball stadium across our nation has its own character and charm. And as it turns out, there are both practical and historical reasons why these unique structural quirks exist and are permitted to continue.

Unlike basketball and football, sports newer to America, baseball has been around since the founding of our nation. As large cities across the country were granted Major League Baseball franchises, city planners first built stadiums inside dense metropolitan areas like the Bronx and Brooklyn, New York, and Philadelphia, Pennsylvania. The stadiums were literally squeezed into existing, crowded city centers. Only two of those great original stadiums still stand, Wrigley Field, home of the Cubs in Chicago, Illinois and Fenway Park, home of the Red Sox in Boston, Massachusetts. As the years passed, and Major League Baseball expanded from 16 teams to the current 30 teams, new stadiums were built to accommodate new franchises, to replace old, out-of-date stadiums, and to entice existing franchises to relocate to new cities. To address both the needs of avid baseball fans and the financial objectives of franchise owners, these new stadiums were built with all modern amenities and structural improvements. For example, new ballparks now have corporate suites and retractable roofs, such as Chase Field in Phoenix, Arizona, home of the Arizona Diamondbacks, and Minute Maid Park in Houston, Texas, home of the Houston Astros. Also, newer stadiums typically offer better food choices, such as fine dining restaurants and improved and strategically placed concessions stations to accommodate their fans. Some even offer vegetarian items on their menus. Finally, many newer stadiums have added baseball-themed fun parks for very young baseball fans to enjoy during their visits to the ballpark. Remarkably, even the world-famous Yankee Stadium, known as "the house that Ruth built," was demolished and in 2009 a new, improved Yankee Stadium was built right next door.

As noted earlier, the only old major league stadiums still in existence are Fenway Park and Wrigley Field. They are beloved by their fans and have become national landmarks. I believe it would be unfair to ask the Red Sox or the Cubs to relocate and probably difficult, if not impossible, for these franchises to dramatically retrofit their iconic stadiums due to their locations in dense urban areas. For this and other reasons, Major League Baseball permits flexible stadium and field dimension rules for all of the teams in the league. As a result, the outfield of every major league stadium has its own unique field dimensions, except for three that share the exact measurements, Kauffman Stadium in Kansas City, Rogers Centre in Toronto, and Dodgers Stadium in Los Angeles.

While the field dimensions and some other aspects of major

league ballparks are all different, each and every of these baseball cathedrals have one thing in common. They are all sacred ground for potential Baseball Gods moments. Like the churches around the world, baseball stadiums have been known to have their share of sacred, and even miraculous, moments.

One such moment occurred on June 25, 2018 at Kauffman Stadium when the Kansas City Royals were hosting the Los Angeles Angels. Right there, in between pitches during the bottom of the seventh inning, an Angles fan dressed in a Mike Trout baseball jersey got down on one knee and proposed to his girlfriend, a Royals fan. The couple had seats right behind home plate so the entire marriage proposal was captured live on television. By the way, she said yes.

While that couple's wedding proposal at Kauffman Stadium was indeed a sacred Baseball Gods moment, just two months later at Comerica Park in Detroit, Michigan, home of the Detroit Tigers, a different kind of sacred moment occurred. On August 16, 2018 world famous singer Aretha Franklin, known as the "Queen of Soul," passed away at the age of 76. Since Franklin began her music career in Detroit, singing in a gospel choir, the Tigers' organization quickly decided to pay tribute to her on that day. Before the Tigers took the field for the game against the visiting Chicago Cubs, the stadium announcer asked for a moment of silence to honor Franklin. At the same time, the stadium scoreboard displayed a photo of Franklin on the big screen together with the words "RESPECT" and "Forever Our Queen." Just as the ballplayers and fans were honoring Franklin's legacy, a large rainbow miraculously appeared above the stadium, right above her photo. No doubt everyone at Comerica Park that day would agree that — The Baseball Gods are real.

CHAPTER FOUR

The Baseball Gods

"The Baseball Gods are testing us."
— Bruce Bochy

MOST RELIGIONS AND RELIGIOUS DEVOTEES WORSHIP A higher power. This higher power is said to be God, believed to be a supreme being that governs and controls the ways of the world. The concept of God, as described by theologians, commonly includes the attributes of an all-knowing, all-powerful, invisible and all-present deity. While the Abrahamic religions are monotheistic, thus believing in just one God, in the religion of baseball, most ballplayers, managers, coaches and fans worship a collection of supreme deities known as — The Baseball Gods.

Sometimes the Baseball Gods are portrayed as kind, loving, and gentle overlords. When good things happen to our favorite team or player, the Baseball Gods are praised for their acts of generosity and benevolence. Other times the Baseball Gods are portrayed as angry and vengeful. When bad things happen to our favorite team or player, the Baseball Gods are held responsible, having forsaken us or even cursed us.

Baseball players who have learned about or experienced the mysterious ways of the Baseball Gods know that it's a good idea to stay in their good graces. When Golden Glove winning outfielder Josh Reddick of the Houston Astros talked about his hot hitting streak in late June of 2017, he vowed not to anger the Baseball Gods. A year later in 2018, after extending his on-base streak, Texas Rangers' outfielder Shin-Soo Choo, in an after-game interview with reporters, thanked the Baseball Gods for "the gift" they bestowed upon him. When I learned about Reddick and Choo's comments, I thought now here are two ballplayers that really get it. Plenty of major league managers get it as well. In 2017, after his San Francisco Giants lost twelve of thirteen games, manager Bruce Bochy told reporters that "the Baseball Gods are testing us."

Many other baseball managers and coaches understand what Bruce Bochy was talking about. One of them, for sure, is Terry Collins, the former manager of the New York Mets. The Mets' organization and their loyal fans had high hopes for a team loaded with talent as they broke spring training camp and began the 2015 campaign. At one point during the long, 162-game season, the Mets had won eleven games in a row, had the best record in baseball, and looked like they were on their way to the playoffs. However, by mid-season the team found themselves in an awful slump. On a beautiful, sunny Thursday afternoon in July, the Cubs defeated the Mets to complete a three-game series sweep. The Mets' offense could generate only one run in those 27 innings against the Cubs. At that point, the Mets had lost ten of fourteen games and their hopes for a spot in the postseason were slowly slipping away.

In Mike Axisa's CBS Sports article entitled "Mets' Collins

After Latest Loss: 'The Only Thing Left is Human Sacrifice,'" the sports writer concluded that Collins was running out of ideas to improve his offense and turn his team around. Collins had jokingly told Axisa and other reporters that the only thing left to do under the circumstances was to find a human sacrifice and he was going to have to pick somebody. Despite Collins' comment, no member of the Mets' 25-man roster went missing during the 2015 season.

Perhaps Collins did sacrifice a chicken, or a goat, or something else because the Mets recovered from their losing streak and went on to make the playoffs. Then they won the National League Conference Championship Series and moved on to play the Kansas City Royals in the 2015 World Series. Given this roller coaster ride, ending with a loss in the World Series, I think Terry Collins and the New York Mets' organization would certainly agree that the Baseball Gods are real and that they had an impact on the Mets' 2015 season.

Although the Mets lost to the Kansas City Royals in the 2015 World Series, their hopes were high entering the 2016 season. The team finished in second place in their division with an 87-75 winning record, eight games behind the league leading Washington Nationals, and made it to the National League playoffs as a Wild Card. However, unlike the Kansas City Royals who were defeated in the 2014 World Series but returned a year later in 2015 to win it all, the Mets fell short in their quest to make it back to baseball's promised land. Despite having home field advantage, the Mets lost to the San Francisco Giants 3-0 in the Wild Card game, with the Giants scoring all three runs in the top of the ninth inning. It was truly a heartbreaker for all Mets' fans.

Despite another setback to end their 2016 season, the Mets' loyal fans still had high hopes for 2017. And there was good reason for their continued enthusiasm. With a returning squad that included young, hard-throwing pitchers Jacob deGrom, Matt Harvey and Noah Syndergaard and a host of talented position players like David Wright and Yoenis Cespedes, the prospects for the Mets going into the season looked pretty good.

But it was not to be. Despite their solid team roster that included many members of the 2015 National League championship team, the 2017 season for the Mets got off to a disappointing start. In May the Mets found themselves in second place in the division, but they were 5 games below .500 with a losing record of 16-21. As the distance between the Mets and the league leading Washington Nationals grew larger, their fans and sports writers sensed something was amiss. Many blamed the Mets' poor win-loss record on injuries, and I have a sense that manager Terry Collins knew who caused those injuries to happen.

On April 2, starting pitcher Steven Matz went on the disabled list for two months with tenderness in his pitching elbow. On May 1, star pitcher Noah Syndergaard went on the DL for months with a torn muscle. Ten days later on May 11, relief pitcher and closer Jeurys Familia underwent surgery to remove a blood clot found near his armpit and did not return to the bullpen for months. And on June 15 another pitcher, Matt Harvey, suffered a stress injury to the scapula bone in his right shoulder and went on the DL for an extended period. Clearly, injuries had decimated the Mets' pitching staff.

As if this wasn't enough, the Mets' team leader and third

baseman David Wright, who had been plagued by injuries most of his career, once again was placed on the DL as the 2017 season began. The herniated disc problem in his neck returned and a serious right shoulder impingement caused Wright to miss the entire season. Four weeks later on April 27, star homerun hitter Yoenis Cespedes also got hurt. He strained his left hamstring running out a double in a game against the Atlanta Braves. It took Cespedes weeks to recover, but he was never the same player he was before the injury. Given these injuries, as well as a host of additional injuries to many other Mets' players, it was no surprise that the Mets' starting rotation and bullpen were performing poorly and the team's run production and batting average, down to .239, were under-performing as well.

At first, Mets' manager Terry Collins tried to keep a positive attitude and stay optimistic doing his best Tony Robbins impression. He tried to keep an upbeat tone and look forward to the new day ahead. He would not blame the team's poor performance on injuries or bad luck, but rather on the team's poor execution of baseball basics. Yet as the losses continued and sports reporters kept nagging Collins with questions after another late inning collapse, his tone changed and he confessed how he really felt by blurting out, "Right now, somebody has pissed off the baseball gods because every move we make, it turns out to be the wrong one, no matter what it is."

While this was happening to the Mets on the field, some sports writers focused on this Baseball Gods theme in print. Sports writer Rob Piersall posted an article on MetsMerizedOnline. com entitled "Terry Collins Laments Loss to Arizona, Blames Baseball Gods." On the same day, I found another article penned by sports writer Jessica Kleinschmidt with the following great title: "Terry Collins Bemoans 'Pissed Off' Baseball Gods as Mets Continue to Crumble." Collins blamed the Baseball Gods in both articles and called them out for his team's bad luck. This might not have been such a good idea.

Just two weeks later, things got so bad for the Mets that sports writers in New York were taking odds on whether Collins would lose his job. In his May 25th article in Sportswatch entitled "Baseball Gods Abusing Mets Manager Terry Collins this Season," Neil Best wrote, "Maybe Terry Collins does not survive the summer, or at the very least, maybe he and the Mets part ways after the season." Best acknowledged that "It's a tough business and a tough town, and Collins already has been around longer than any other Mets manager in history and does not have a World Series ring to show for it."

Terry Collins was a veteran manager whose managerial career began two decades earlier in 1993 with the Houston Astros. He had been around the block, and the baseball diamond, a time or two. 2017 was not his first disappointing losing season and not his first run-in with the Baseball Gods. But the Baseball Gods were severely unkind to Collins and the Mets in 2017. In fact, Mets' players spent more than 1,100 days on the disable list that year. And as Neil Best predicted, Collins "retired" as the manager of the Mets immediately after the final out in their final game of the 2017 season.

Another franchise that probably believes in the Baseball Gods is the Cleveland Indians. Their bond with the Baseball Gods may have been formed in 1989 when the sports comedy film *Major League* was released. The film, written and directed by David S. Ward with an outstanding cast including Tom

Berenger, Charlie Sheen, Wesley Snipes, James Gammon, Rene
Russo, Dennis Haysbert and Corbin Bernson, is a fictionalized
version of one season of the Cleveland Indians major league
baseball team.

As the film begins, we learn that the team owner has died
and the franchise has been inherited by his wife, Rachel Phelps,
a former Las Vegas showgirl dancer, now a very wealthy
widow. Phelps hates the city of Cleveland and is determined
to move the Indians to a warm city like Miami, Florida. She
finds out there is a loophole in the Indians' contract with the
city of Cleveland which stipulates that if the season attendance
drops below a certain level, the team can opt out of its deal
and relocate.

To accomplish this objective, Phelps decides to build the
worst baseball team of all time. She proceeds to hire a manager
and coaches with losing track records and recruits a motley
crew of the worst ballplayers, guys that no other teams want,
to build their roster. The team's third baseman, Roger Dorn,
is an egotistical has-been whose skills have faded. The team's
pitching ace is a washed-up hurler named Eddie Harris. The
veteran catcher, Jake Taylor, is so far over the hill that he spent
the last few seasons playing baseball in the Mexican League.
Taylor's knees are so bad that he has to ice them after every
practice and his arm strength is so weak that he can't even
reach second base to throw out a runner trying to steal the
base. Then there is voodoo, Jobu-worshipping Pedro Cerrano,
a power hitting Cuban refugee who can crush a fastball but
everyone knows can't hit a curveball. Two young ballplayers
are recruited but their shortcomings exceed their potential.
The first, Willie Mays Hayes, is super-fast but can't get on

base. The second is Ricky Vaughn, nicknamed "Wild Thing," a former convicted felon on a work release from a California prison. Vaughn, who becomes the most popular player on the team, earned his nickname because he has an unhittable fastball but can't control it.

Sure enough, as the season grinds on, the losses pile up and Indians are the team with the worst record in baseball. As expected, the fans stop supporting the team and attendance at the stadium declines precipitously. Rachel Phelps' master plan was coming together.

Of course, *Major League* is a Hollywood movie and the plot takes a turn. The players learn of Phelps' evil scheme and implement a plan of their own. With nothing left to lose, they have a team meeting in the clubhouse and agree to dedicate themselves to playing well and winning like never before. The clubhouse chemistry improves and the players come together as a team. Each player overcomes his personal problems and shortcomings and the Indians start to win games. Despite Phelps' continuing efforts to prevent the team from succeeding, the Indians win enough games to find themselves into contention for the division championship. The season ends with the Indians tied with the New York Yankees in first place, which forces a one-game playoff to determine the winner.

As if the film's screenwriter and director were familiar with the power of the Baseball Gods, it all comes together for the Indians during the playoff game against the Yankees. Willie Mays Hayes steals a base! Pedro Cerrano finally hits a curveball and knocks it out of the park for a home run to tie the game! In the ninth inning, with two outs, the bases loaded, and the Indians in the lead, the Indians manager waves in "Wild

Thing" Ricky Vaughn from the bullpen. As Vaughn strolls in toward the pitcher's mound, we hear his now famous walkout song "Wild Thing," written by Chip Taylor, blasting out of the stadium speakers, with the crowd cheering and singing along with the song. Vaughn, now wearing corrective eyeglasses to improve his vision, strikes out the batter with three straight fastballs and the Indians win the division championship!

As a result of his game-ending strikeout to close out the game, Ricky Vaughn receives most of the accolades and gets to do the post-game interview. However, it's the team's power hitting, voodoo-practicing, Cuban import Pedro Cerrano who may be the real most valuable player of the game. And, in my opinion, he is clearly the most interesting personality on the team and has some of the best one-liners in the film. For example, in the center of his locker, Cerrano built a shrine for Jobu, his small voodoo doll. Jobu has white hair, a cigar in his mouth, wears a white robe with a red sash around his waist, and wears fancy necklaces. He's a funny looking idol indeed. Every day Cerrano prays to Jobu and brings him sacrifices asking for his help to hit the curveball. In one of the many humorous scenes in the movie Cerrano speaks to Jobu and says, "Bats, they are sick. I cannot hit curveball. Straight ball I hit very much. Curveball, bats are afraid. I ask Jobu to come, take fear from bats. I offer him cigar, rum. He will come." Some of my favorite Cerrano one-line quotes include; "Have to wake up bat!" "Hats for bats, keep bats warm," "Is very bad to steal Jobu's rum. Is very bad."

As the movie advances towards its climax, Cerrano finally realizes that he must look within for help, not to Jobu or the heavens. He decides to believe in himself and, right before he smashes the game-tying home run, declares, "I'm pissed off now, Jobu. Look, I go to you. I stick up for you. You no help me now. I say . . . Jobu, I do it myself." In this context, the movie demonstrates that the power of positive thinking and believing in yourself can be helpful in achieving your goals.

In 2016, almost three decades after its release, *Major League* and Jobu resurfaced at Progressive Field, the home stadium of the real Cleveland Indians. At the time, the Indians had a 27-24 record and were falling in the standings in the Central Division, in third place behind the division leading Kansas City Royals and the Chicago White Sox. They were in a slump. Looking to turn things around, the team turned to Jobu. Veterans Jason Kipnis and Mike Napoli built a shrine for Jobu between their lockers, just as Pedro Cerrano had done in the movie. This shrine featured two statues of Jobu, with mini-bottles of rum, and a wool sweater with a picture of Jobu on it and an inscription that read "It is very bad to drink Jobu's rum. Very bad."

When journalist Kate Feldman of the New York Daily News heard what was going on in the team's clubhouse, she wrote an article entitled "Cleveland Indians Erect Jobu Shrine from 'Major League' Film in Clubhouse." In the article she interviews Kipnis, who tells her, "He's been working. He didn't like the first airport vodka we left him. So we tried Bacardi (rum) and that seems to be working." Familiar with one of the unwritten rules of baseball, Kipnis said, "Right now it's working so we're not going to mess with what works." Coincidence or not, Cleveland went on a six-game winning streak and just a few weeks later found themselves in first place in the Central Division, three games ahead of the Kansas City Royals.

By mid-July, the Indians had a six and a half game lead in

the division and had the best record in the American League. Everything was going right for Cleveland except one thing. Yan Gomes, the team's catcher, was batting a mere .163 and was in a terrible season-long slump. After a team meeting, the clubhouse leaders did something that Mets' Manager Terry Collins would likely have approved. Kipnis, Napoli, Lonnie Chisenhall and Chris Gimenez decided to build a shrine and make a sacrifice to the Baseball Gods to break Gomez out of his slump.

The four teammates carefully planned a ceremony to please the Baseball Gods. The shrine was a makeshift altar with a white robe for Gomes to wear, a bouquet of flowers, a piñata filled with candy, a baseball bat, and a chicken to be sacrificed. The ceremony started with a blessing from team leader Napoli, who was wearing a rainbow cape for the occasion. Surrounded by the team, with his hand on Gomes' head, Napoli said, "We have prepared this exorcism to honor the holiness and to absolve Yan Gomes of any wrongdoing that he may have committed towards thee. We urge you to forgive his obsession with the octagon and bestow him with your guidance and grace on the diamond. Please accept these offerings as atonement for him straying from the righteous path. Be kind and just in your willingness to accept him and not condemn him any further. In the name of Jobu, amen." After Napoli pleaded his case to the Baseball Gods, Gomes sacrificed the chicken, grabbed the baseball bat and attacked the piñata with all his might. To conclude the ceremony, Kipnis said, "May the hits be plenty."

Cleveland finished the season with ninety-four wins. They won the Central Division and made it all the way to the World

Series. Although they did lose the series to the Chicago Cubs, 8-7 in 10 innings in Game 7, I am confident that Napoli, Kipnis and the rest of the 2016 Cleveland Indians would agree that the Baseball Gods are real.

The Cleveland Indians were not the only baseball team to create an idol for the Baseball Gods in recent years. The next year, another series would take place before the beginning of the 2017 baseball season. This would be the World Baseball Classic; an international professional competition held every four years and is the equivalent to the World Cup in soccer. Much to the surprise of all who follow baseball, it was the team from Israel that qualified for the World Classic, and they were the team that created an idol, more like a mascot, to help them play well.

By way of background, Israel is a very small country about the size of the state of New Jersey with a population of about only 9 million residents. And it doesn't have too many baseball fields. The Israeli national team didn't even have enough professional baseball players to fill a roster. So, they got creative. They completed the team with essentially unknown minor league baseball players of Jewish heritage from the United States. Just like the Jamaican bobsled team that became a worldwide sensation during the Winter Olympics in 1998 and the Icelandic soccer team in the 2018 World Cup competition, Israel ranked #41 in the world baseball ratings and was the biggest underdog at the 2017 World Baseball Classic. To make matters more challenging, they had to play against Great Britain, Brazil, and Pakistan, all higher-ranked teams, to qualify for the main draw of the competition. Israel played great and defeated them all.

As they entered the main draw of the competition, the Israeli team had momentum and their spirits were high. In the first round of the tournament, the underdog "Jew Crew," the team's new nickname, had to face South Korea, ranked #3 in the world, Chinese Taipei, ranked #4, and the Netherlands, ranked #9. Again, Israel played great, defeated them all, and moved on to the second round of the main draw competition.

Perhaps the biggest surprise was team Israel's 2-1 defeat of South Korea, one of the favorites to win the event. During the press conference after that game, baseball fans around the world learned why Israel played so well. They had a secret spiritual weapon, the "Mensch on a Bench," that helped them win the game.

Former Hasbro toy executive and author Neal Hoffman is the man behind the "Mensch on the Bench." Hoffmann created the Mensch, a stuffed doll named Moshe that looks like a rabbi, and introduced Moshe as the lead character in a storybook to engage children with the story of Hanukkah. The Mensch concept exploded shortly thereafter when Hoffmann pitched his creation to the entrepreneurs on Shark Tank, the popular TV reality show. The Mensch has become a sales phenomenon ever since. Just Google it and see for yourself.

Getting back to baseball, sports writer Jeff Eisenband high-lighted Moshe the Mensch in his *The Post Game* article "Meet 'Mensch on a Bench,' Israel's Cuddly World Baseball Classic Mascot." He explained that "mensch" is a Yiddish word that means "a good person." In Eisenband's article, ESPN's senior sports writer Eddie Matz, referencing Moshe, is quoted saying, "He's essentially the Jewish answer to 'Elf on the Shelf.'" Matz noted that to the guys in the Israeli team clubhouse, Moshe was much more than a toy doll. For the ballplayers, he was a spiritual figure. Like Jobu in *Major League*, the Mensch on the Bench had his own locker in the clubhouse, which the players turned into a shrine in recognition of his importance.

At that same press conference after the game against South Korea, Israel team leader Cody Decker showed up with a large doll version of the "Mensch on a Bench" and sat him down right next to him during the interview. When asked about the Mensch, Decker said, "He's a mascot, he's a friend, he's a teammate, he's a borderline deity to our team... He brings a lot to the table." Decker continued, "He is everywhere and nowhere all at once. His actual location is irrelevant because he exists in higher metaphysical planes. But he's always near."

The producers of *Major League* must have been pleased with Cody Decker when he said of the Mensch, "Every team needs their Jobu. He was ours. He had his own locker, and we gave him offerings: Manischewitz, gelt and gefitle fish."

Given the series of surprising events described in this chapter, I think Cody Decker, Team Israel, Mike Napoli, Jason Kipnis, Yan Gomes, Bruce Bochy and Terry Collins, would agree that the Baseball Gods are real.

CHAPTER FIVE

The Baseball Miracles

"I am realistic, I expect miracles."
—Dr. Wayne Dyer

A MIRACLE CAN BE PERCEIVED AS A NUMBER OF DIFFER-ent things. Some might say a surprising, welcomed event, not explainable by natural or scientific laws and is therefore considered work of the divine, is a miracle. Others might consider a highly improbable or extraordinary event that brings very welcomed consequences a miracle. In the religion of baseball, we have come to expect miracles because they happen all the time.

Every year since 1909, the annual Congressional Baseball Game for Charity is played in the Alexandria, Virginia suburb of Washington, D.C. between Republicans and Democrats. During practice before the next day's game in June of 2017, a crazed gunman with a rifle stormed the ballfield. Republican Steve Scalise, House Majority Whip at that time, was playing second base on that fateful day. While manning his position, bullets shots exploded and one of them entered Scalise's hip and traveled through his body. Due to the direction of the bullet, tremendous damage was done as the bullet tore muscle and bone, which caused extensive, out-of-control bleeding. As he laid on the ground with bullets still whizzing through the air, Representative Scalise was in imminent risk of death.

Scott Barkley described the scene in his June 15th article "Georgia Congressman: '…God was on That Baseball Field'":

> Georgia District 11 Representative Barry Loudermilk stood near the batter's box Wednesday morning when the first shots rang out. Moments later he was joining others, seeking cover from a gunman who would shoot five people, including two police officers and House Majority Whip Steve Scalise. Scalise, struck in the hip while standing near second base, could only manage to drag himself to the outfield. Meanwhile, the shooting continued between the gunman and responding law enforcement for ten minutes. Loudermilk told Atlanta's Fox5 News, "If it wasn't for them it would have been a killing field out there today. We are very blessed that God was on that baseball field."

Congressman Loudermilk was not the only member of Congress to refer to God's intervention that day. Journalist Kirk Brown recounts the tragic events in his August 29th article "Duncan Credits 'God Wink' for Protecting Him from Gunman at GOP Baseball Practice."

South Carolina Representative Jeff Duncan said Monday night that a "God wink" protected him from a gunman who opened fire on the GOP. "I was on the congressional baseball team that was targeted by an assassin," Duncan said at his annual Faith & Freedom barbecue fundraiser at the Anderson Civic Center. "God was looking after your congressman. God got me off that field beforehand, but not before I met the shooter face-to-face and looked him in the eye as he asked me who was practicing that morning." Duncan was driven to the team's practice on the morning of June 14th by his scheduler, Thomas McCallister. Duncan said for some reason McCallister backed his pickup into a parking space which prevented gunman James Hodgkinson from seeing the "Duncan for Congress" sticker on the vehicle's rear bumper. According to Duncan, his name was on a list that the attacker had in his pocket when they spoke in front of McCallister's pickup. If McCallister had pulled into the parking space, Duncan said, Hodgkinson "may have put two and two together and recognized me and possibly could have begun his act of violence right there in the parking lot." "It was a God wink," Duncan said.

After several surgeries and a difficult recovering, Representative Scalise surprisingly returned to Congress just fifteen weeks after he was shot. He addressed his House chamber colleagues for the first time since the shooting and rejoiced, "I'm definitely a living example that miracles really do happen."

Later that year, the Washington Nationals made the play-offs and hosted the Chicago Cubs in the National League Division Series. The honor of throwing out the ceremonial first pitch for Game 1 of that series was given to none other than the inspirational House Majority Whip Steve Scalise. The Baseball Gods must have been pleased to play a role in this miracle.

Baseball miracles take place everywhere, from a local park ballfield in Alexandria, Virginia to the professional spring training ballfields of the Arizona Fall Baseball League. That is where 2007 Heisman Trophy winner, college football legend, and former National Football League player Tim Tebow made his October 12, 2016 debut as a baseball player for the New York Mets. After the game, fan favorite Tebow was signing autographs when another baseball miracle took place. As described in an article written by Josh Peter on the same day, a fan suffered an apparent seizure while Tebow was signing autographs. Tebow went to the aid of the fan, put his hands on the man, and started praying. Shortly thereafter, the fan miraculously regained consciousness. In his first public comments about the incident, Tebow, a devout Christian, said, "As far as me and miracles, no, . . . But in the God that we serve, yeah, I do believe in miracles." Tebow added, "I don't know what the situation was, but I know that the God that I get to serve is the God that is always performing miracles in people's lives every day, all the time. As a Christian, that's the hope that we get to live by, . . . we get to serve a God that does amazing things every single day . . . It's one of the greatest hopes you get to live with."

Perhaps a miracle of lesser magnitude, in Tim Tebow's first at bat as a minor leaguer in the Mets' organization, he hit a two-run home run. That's right, the same guy who may have saved a man's life after a game in 2016, hit a home run during his first professional at-bat in 2017. Tebow led his new team, the South Carolina Fireflies, to a 14-7 victory over the visiting Augusta GreenJackets that day. Journalist Ron Dicker's descriptive *Huffington Post* article of the day's events had the most fitting title: "Tim Tebow Homers in Minor League Season Debut, Miracles May Never Cease." The Baseball Gods must love Tim Tebow.

Another baseball miracle of a totally different nature took place years ago further out west, in the seats of Dodgers Stadium. As the story goes, in August 2003 Juan Catalan, a 24-year-old father who worked in his family's machining business, was arrested for the murder of a 16-year-old girl who had testified in a gang murder case. Catalan said that he was wrongly accused and had a rock-solid alibi for the murder. He claimed that he and his 6-year-old daughter were at Dodger Stadium to see the Dodgers play the Atlanta Braves at the time of the murder. Catalan even produced the ticket stub for the game as proof, but to no avail. He was sent to jail to await trial for capital murder.

Thereafter, Catalan remembered that a TV show was being filmed that night at the ballpark and he recalled being caught on tape. It turned out he was right. It was an episode of the very popular Larry David comedy series *Curb Your Enthusiasm*. Video footage from the show provided the proof that Catalan and his defense attorney, Todd Melnick, needed to prove his innocence. The tape, filmed at Dodgers Stadium that night shows Catalan in the stands eating a hot dog, watching the game, and later he and his daughter leaving the game in the ninth inning, just as he proclaimed while trying to prove his case.

Juan Catalan's story is told in vivid detail in the true crime documentary *Long Shot*, which aired on Netflix years later in 2017. Catalan appears in the documentary as do members of his family and Larry David as well. I'm pretty sure that

Catalan, a man accused of murder who had his innocence proven only because of the coincidental help of Larry David's film crew at a Los Angeles Dodgers baseball game, thought this was a miracle.

While Juan Catalan was saving his own life from a lifetime in prison, Bubba Derby, a pitcher with the Milwaukee Brewers organization and former Biloxi Shucker teammate of my ex-colleague Jon Perrin, spent an evening during the offseason of 2017 saving the lives of others. Derby travelled with some family members to the *Route 91 Harvest Country Music Festival* in Las Vegas, Nevada. On October 1, 2017, a night when hundreds of concertgoers were looking forward to a great night of music, 58 people tragically lost their lives in a mass shooting. In his article entitled "Brewers Prospect Bubba Derby Heroically Shielded Others with His Body During Las Vegas Shooting," Zachary Ripple tried to find something uplifting about that evening when he wrote:

> In the tragic mass shooting in Las Vegas over the weekend, several heroes emerged as they protected others from the gunfire. Milwaukee Brewers minor leaguer Bubba Derby was among those, selflessly blocking two young women he had met at the Route 91 Harvest Festival with his own body as bullets rained down . . . "I turned and looked at my aunt, who was behind me," said Derby in a video interview as he recounted the horrifying events of the weekend. "And I remember looking at her eyes and it was that look of, 'Are we about to die? Is this it for us?'... Derby, 23, went on to explain that he tried to shield the two young women he had met by

covering them with his body, as his brother did the same for his girlfriend… "You could hear the bullets ricocheting off the ground."

While losing so many souls so senselessly was yet another heartbreaking tragedy at the hands of a deranged gunman, perhaps it was a miracle that so many music fans made it out alive that night. No doubt the Baseball Gods are proud of Bubba Derby.

Another baseball player whose heroic efforts are surely celebrated by the Baseball Gods is that of Roberto Clemente. Clemente, born in Puerto Rico, played all of his 18 seasons with the Pittsburgh Pirates during which time he was an All-Star 12 times, the National League Most Valuable Player in 1966, the league batting champ 4 times, and the winner of 12 consecutives Golden Glove Awards for his outstanding defense in right field. He was inducted into the Baseball Hall of Fame in 1973 as the first Latin played ever to be inducted.

Based on my research for this book, I believe that Roberto Clemente, perhaps even more importantly, also earned a spot in the hall of fame of humanity. He spent much of his time during the off-season involved in charity work. He was known as a humanitarian and hero for these off-field endeavors. Tragically, Clemente died in a plane crash while on his way to deliver food and supplies to suffering earthquake victims in Nicaragua.

I was fascinated to learn that Clemente's lifetime of humanitarian work and his more recent connection to a medical miracle may soon earn him sainthood. The story is described in detail in Marissa Payne's *Washington Post* article published on August 17, 2017 entitled "After July 'Miracle' Pope Francis Reportedly Moves Roberto Clemente Close to Sainthood."

The tale began a year earlier in 2016 when former Olympic high jumper Jamie Nieto was injured. Nieto, then a coach, was attempting to perform a back-flip, his signature move during his competitive years, but he slipped, broke his neck, and was partially paralyzed from his neck down. According to Payne, Nieto was given a slim chance by doctors to regain enough strength and mobility in his legs to ever walk again. However, he proved them wrong. The Olympian, who had proposed to Jamaican hurdler Shevon Stoddart while still in his wheelchair just six months after his accident, took 130 nearly unaided, miraculous steps at his wedding.

Nieto, who coincidentally portrayed Roberto Clemente in the film *Baseball's Last Hero*, credited his recovery to hard work and determination. However, according to Richard Rossi, the director of *Baseball's Last Hero*, Nieto's miracle recovery was attributable to the spirit of Roberto Clemente. His proof, as reported by the Christian Newswire, was documented in a letter he had written to Pope Francis. According to Payne's article, "In meditation, it was revealed to me that Roberto Clemente was a saint," Richard Rossi wrote. "I saw a miracle healing of Jamie Nieto. He will walk at his own wedding to show the grace of the sacrament of marriage." According to Rossi, who began his campaign to make Clemente a saint in 2014, this is not the first miracle to occur in Clemente's name. Rossi also contends that Clemente, a devout Catholic, also performed miracles while he was alive. Shortly thereafter, because of the belief that Roberto Clemente had met the requirement of performing a miracle, Pope Francis officially declared Clemente "blessed." With this Papal beatification, the Catholic Church says that Clemente, the Hall of Fame baseball player and great humanitarian, has just one step left in order to become a "saint."

While I was writing this chapter about baseball miracles, the Soccer Gods were busy creating a miracle of their own in Southeast Asia. On a typical day in June in Thailand, twelve boys aged eleven to sixteen and their 25-year-old assistant coach, Ekapol Chantawong, decided to explore a cave as a fun activity after their soccer practice. The boys, who played for the Wild Boars football team, headed deep within the dark Tham Luang cave complex in Chiang Rai Province. Unbeknown to these explorers, outside the cave monsoon rains began to deluge the area. The water levels in the cave began to rise and the boys and their coach became trapped deep inside. Chantawong, a former Buddhist monk, decided that the team should go deeper into the cave to find a safer place to avoid the rising waters and rest for the night. The heavy rains and flooding continued and kept them all underground in the cave for the next 17 days.

Thai Navy Seals were initially tasked with rescuing the soccer team. They were assisted by almost 1,000 rescue experts from around the world who came to help. The daring rescue operation, which received global news coverage, was a success in that all the boys and the coach survived. Unfortunately, two members of rescue teams lost their lives.

There were many heroes outside the cave who helped save the boys. There was also a hero inside the cave, assistant coach Ekapol Chantawong. When he was just ten years old, Chantawong's entire village was ravaged and wiped out by a disease. He was the only one to survive. He lost both of his parents and his brother. His extended family from another village decided to send him to a Buddhist temple for training to be a monk. He spent ten years as a monk and learned many things, including how to meditate. While trapped in the cave, Chantawong dug down deep into his experience as a monk and taught the boys how to meditate. And together they prayed for rescue. When a pair of British divers finally found Chantawong and the boys, the children were not screaming or crying. Instead, they were sitting quietly in the dark, peacefully meditating. After being rescued, Adul Sam-on, the only boy on the team that spoke English, said, "It was a miracle."

I'm confident that, based on the miracles described in this chapter, House Representatives Steve Scalise, Barry Loudermilk and Jeff Duncan, and Tim Tebow, Juan Catalan, Bubba Derby and Jamie Nieto would all agree that the Baseball Gods are real. Of course, in the case of Coach Ekapol Chantawong and Adul Sam-on, it's the Soccer Gods that are real.

CHAPTER SIX

The Baseball Gods Moments

"One last game of catch at home with my dad."
—Drew Blake

I THINK "BASEBALL GODS" MOMENTS ARE SYNCHRONIS-tic, poetic and serendipitous events that take place on the field or around the game of baseball. Some of these moments are uplifting, like Willie Mays' famous over-the-shoulder catch during Game 1 of the 1954 World Series between the New York Giants and the Cleveland Indians. Some are not, like Billy Buckner's unfortunate fielding error during Game 6 of the 1986 World Series between the Boston Red Sox and the New York Mets. And other Baseball Gods moments are intended to teach a valuable lesson. In these instances, these moments can be viewed as karma.

The Baseball Gods moment for left-handed hitting outfielder Dustin Fowler had a little bit of everything. He was a top pros-pect, he incurred a freak injury, he was involved in a trade, and the first major league base hit of his career was coinciden-tal and serendipitous. Fowler was selected in the eighteenth round in the 2013 draft by the New York Yankees. Four years into his professional baseball career, he got called up to "the show," the major leagues, something many kids dream about as soon as he has his first catch with his dad. Fowler made his pro debut on June 29, 2017 on the road against the Chicago White Sox. Unfortunately, his dream come true abruptly turned into a nightmare.

Maybe it was a warning from the Baseball Gods when the start of the game was delayed three hours due to rain, surely an ominous beginning. Perhaps the wet field conditions played a role in what took place shortly thereafter. In right field, in just the second inning of his major league debut, Fowler ran fast and hard to catch a fly ball that was curving into foul territory. As he hustled toward the right field wall to make the catch, Fowler tripped as he reached for the ball and fell over the railing into the stands. He was injured, in considerable pain, and had to be carted off the field. What made this a "freak injury" was that there was an unpadded, unsecured electrical box on the ground near the right field wall that caused Fowler to trip.

The X-ray at the hospital revealed a rupture of Fowler's right patellar tendon. The injury would require surgery and, as a result, he received the bad news that he would be out for the remainder of the season. Sadly, Fowler's rookie season as a New York Yankee in the big leagues ended after less than two innings of play. He never even got one at bat at the plate.

Near the end of the 2017 season, the Yankees were looking to improve their team for a playoff run. Fowler, still on the injured reserve list, was packaged in a trade deal. The Yankees sent Fowler and teammates James Kaprielian and Jorge Mateo to the Oakland Athletics in exchange for pitcher Sonny Gray.

After the grueling rehabilitation process, Fowler was healthy, ready to play, and had a fresh start with his new team as he entered the 2018 season. Unfortunately, he began the season with the A's back in the minor leagues playing for their Triple-A team, the Nashville Sounds. In 132 plate appearances, Fowler recorded a very respectable .310 batting average with three home runs and eight steals. The combination of speed, power, and solid batting average earned him another call-up to the major leagues. Believe it or not, Fowler made his Oakland A's debut against, you guessed it, the New York Yankees. Even more surprising, Fowler's first career plate appearance was against Sonny Gray, the very same starting pitcher he was traded for the year before. I wonder if the Baseball Gods had something to do with this coincidence. For the record, Fowler struck out in his first career at-bat. However, in his next at bat in the top of the fourth inning, he hit a single, logging his long awaited first career base hit as a major league ballplayer.

Some Baseball Gods moments are related to base hits, like Dustin Fowler's, or to home runs, like Bobby Thompson's "shot heard around the world." And sometimes they come in bizarre ways, such as with a balk. For those unfamiliar with the balk rule (8.05 of the rules of Major League Baseball), a balk is an illegal act by the pitcher with a runner or runners on base entitling all runners to advance one base. The balk rule is complex and technical, with thirteen different actions that constitute a balk.

During 2018, the Eugene Emeralds, the Oregon-based Class A minor league affiliate of the Chicago Cubs, was having a terrible first half of the season. The team had the worst record in the Northwest League. However, league rules state that a team can qualify for the year-end playoffs based solely on its second-half performance. So even though their overall record was mediocre at best, the Emeralds played just well enough in the second half of the season to make the playoffs. Then the team got really hot and went on a winning streak. In fact, the Emeralds went undefeated in the playoffs, winning each game with a late inning comeback. After five playoff wins in a row, they found themselves in the championship game.

So there they were, in the championship game, with the bases loaded and the game tied at two in the bottom of the ninth inning. As the batter was getting ready for the first pitch, Emmanuel Clase, the all-star closer for the other team, accidentality dropped the ball on the pitcher's mound and got called for a balk. Per the balk rules, the runner on third base got to advance to home scoring the winning run of the game. Amazingly, the Eugene Emeralds, the worst team in the league for half the season, somehow became the Northwest League champions because of a balk. That had to be a Baseball Gods moment.

2018 was filled with Baseball Gods moments. Take, for example, the case of a 9-year-old boy named Hunter Gillett whose story was covered by Fox Sports Arizona. Hunter travelled to Philadelphia with his father to consult with orthopedic specialists on reconstructive surgery for his hip dysplasia. To cheer his son up, Hunter's father took him to see the Phillies play against the visiting Arizona Diamondbacks, Hunter's favorite team. Prior to the game, Hunter and his dad got the attention of Diamondbacks' catcher Alex Avila. Avila invited Hunter and his dad onto the field and asked Hunter to choose a bat out of three he was holding to use that night. Hunter selected a bat and the Baseball Gods did the rest. Avila went 3-for-4 that night, including a home run.

There was more to Hunter Gillett's special night. Before the game, he also got to take a photo with the bat of Jarrod Dyson, Avila's Diamondbacks teammate at the time. Perhaps Hunter and the Baseball Gods gave both bats good luck because Dyson, who is best known for his speed, stealing bases and great defense, also hit a home run that night.

This was not the first time a baseball player met a sick kid and then hit a home run. There is a legendary folk story about the great Babe Ruth hitting two home runs for a child who was seriously ill after promising to do so. The tall tale was actually proven to be true when it was documented in the book, *Babe & the Kid*, written by Charlie Poekel.

As the story is told, 11-year-old Johnny Sylvester, who lived in Essex Fells, New Jersey, had a tragic accident when he was thrown off of a horse during the summer of 1926. The accident caused inflammation near his brain, a potentially deadly illness. According to the legendary tale, Johnny told his dad that the only thing that could cheer him up would be a baseball from the World Series between the New York Yankees and the St. Louis Cardinals. Johnny's father asked a well-connected friend for help and a few days later Johnny received a baseball signed by Babe Ruth in the mail. Inscribed on the ball was a special message to Johnny from the Babe: "I'll knock a homer for you in Wednesday's game." The "sultan of swat" came through for Johnny and hit not just one, but two home runs, in that World Series game. When Ruth went to visit Johnny in his hospital bed after the World Series, and Johnny thereafter fully recovered from his illness, the story hoisted the Babe into legendary status.

While Babe Ruth gets almost all of the historical credit for the "Johnny Sylvester Baseball Gods moment," in my opinion there is another aspect of the tale that deserve as much, if not more recognition. Perhaps the most meaningful part of the story was the loving bond between a father, a son, and the great game of baseball.

The next Baseball Gods moment includes another father and his son. Fairfield University senior Drew Blake was playing in the last game of his college baseball career in 2018 when the Baseball Gods made sure that he went out in style. Drew's father just had a feeling that Drew was going to hit the ball out of the park. So, rather than watch the last at bat of his son's college baseball career from the stands with family and friends, he made his way out beyond the outfield fence and positioned himself right behind the right-center field wall, just like a seasoned ballhawk. Perhaps the Baseball Gods told Drew's dad exactly where to stand because his son crushed a deep ball to, you guessed it, right-center field. The right fielder could only watch as the baseball soared over the fence.

Drew Blake, in his last plate appearance as a college baseball player, ended his career by hitting a home run. And he did not just hit a home run. He hit a home run to the exact spot where his father was standing, and his dad made the catch. It was unbelievable! As Drew trotted around the bases to celebrate, he pointed to his father standing beyond the right outfield wall and gave him a salute.

Sports reporter Matt Monagan wrote about the special Blake family Baseball Gods moment in his article "In the Final Home Game of His Career, This College Senior Hit a HR Right into His Dad's Arms." When asked about the home run,

Drew commented, it was "the coolest moment in my sports career." Then, likely thinking back to all of the father-son catches he had throughout his childhood, he said, "One last game of catch at home with my dad."

I think that after all of the Baseball Gods moments described in this chapter, Dustin Fowler, the Eugene Emeralds, Hunter Gillett, Johnny Sylvester, and Drew Blake would agree that the Baseball Gods are Real.

CHAPTER SEVEN

The Holy Spirit

"Now to him who is able to do immeasurably more than all we ask or imagine, according to his power that is at work within us, to him be glory in the church and in Christ Jesus, throughout all generations, forever and ever! Amen."

— Ephesians 3:20-21

WHILE TIM TEBOW BEGAN HIS PROFESSIONAL BASEBALL career with a home run, Hall of Fame catcher Johnny Bench ended his career with one. Johnny Bench's career was legendary from the start. First, he won the rookie of the year at age twenty with the Cincinnati Reds. Individually, Bench won ten consecutive gold glove awards. Then, Bench went on to win four pennants and back-to-back World Series championships with the Cincinnati Reds. Bench, who spent his entire career playing for the Reds and was a key member on the winning Reds teams of the 1970's nicknamed "The Big Red Machine."

In 1983, Johnny Bench announced that it would be his last season. Already a living legend in Ohio, the Reds planned a "Johnny Bench Night" at Cincinnati's Riverfront Stadium before the team played the Houston Astros. In his last game ever, the Baseball Gods made sure that he went out with a bang. The Astros were leading the Reds 2-0 in the bottom of the third when Bench came up to bat. He rose to the occasion and hit a two-run home run, the 389th of his career!

Many Baseball Gods moments could be attributed to a player's biochemistry such surge in adrenaline before an intense moment, but other times I think the holy spirit at work. As depicted in the movie *Angels in the Infield*, if a person has faith in a higher power, then the holy spirit can more easily flow through that individual. When the prana, chi or the holy spirit is flowing through an athlete, special things can happen. Moreover, when an athlete is channeling the holy spirit, he or she can get "in the zone." And when a baseball player gets "in the zone," for all the right reasons, the Baseball Gods are more than eager to assist. Let's start with the example of pitcher Edinson Volquez.

Edinson Volquez was an important pitcher in the Kansas City Royals rotation during their 2014 and 2015 winning seasons. During that time with the Royals, Edinson became good friends with fellow Royals pitcher Yordano Ventura. The business of baseball got in the way of their friendship, and after becoming a free agent after the World Series victory, Volquez signed with the Miami Marlins. In September of 2016, Volquez's new teammate, Miami Marlins pitcher José Fernández, died in a tragic boat accident off the coast of Florida. It was devasting news for the MLB community. During the offseason, in January of 2017, Royals pitcher and Volquez's dear friend Yordano Ventura died tragically in a car accident in the Dominican Republic. Volquez had now lost two friends in a very short period of time.

Edinson Volquez was scheduled to pitch for the Miami Marlins on the birthday of his late friend and fellow pitcher Yordano Ventura on June 3, 2017. It would have been Yordano's twenty-sixth birthday. That morning, Volquez posted on Instagram a photo of himself with Ventura when they were both Kansas City Royals. Edinson wrote how he missed Yordano. As Volquez entered the clubhouse later that day, a member of the Marlins staff walked by Volquez and told him that he would pitch a no-hitter that day. These words would prove to be prophetic.

As Volquez toed the mound to start the game, Volquez was full of emotion and also the holy spirit. The first batter of the day hit a grounder down the first base line, and Edinson Volquez ran to first base to make the play by catching the toss from first baseman Justin Bour. However, batter Reymond Fuentes was running to first with all his might and proceeded to collide with Volquez. While Volquez made the play and got the out, he apparently tweaked his ankle on the play. Volquez was in considerable pain. The game had just started.

Perhaps at that moment, the Baseball Gods came to help Edinson Volquez, because despite the ankle injury, he played on and found that sacred place that few ballplayers ever get to visit called "the zone." Volquez stayed in the zone for nine innings, and batter after batter, he kept getting batters out. Groundballs. Pop Outs. Volquez also racked up ten strike-outs. When the Marlins defeated the Arizona Diamondbacks 3-0, Volquez came to the realization that he had just pitched a no-hitter!

After the game, Edinson Volquez proclaimed to reporters, "This was for Ventura and Jose." The Baseball Gods were likely very proud of Volquez when he told reporters, "Everybody loved Jose. I can say that's for him, too. I really appreciate what he did here and people loved him. I'm really blessed to throw a no-hitter on his bump. I was pretty close to Ventura. To do something like I did, that's really special for me to dedicate the game to him. It was one of those days you wake up and don't really know what's going to happen. Next thing you know, you have a no-hitter." The holy spirit flowed into Edinson Volquez that night, just like it flowed into Miami Marlins second baseman Dee Gordon the first game the Marlins played after the death of teammate José Fernández.

The Miami Marlins and their fans paid tribute to José Fernández before the first game after his passing. In his honor, every Marlins player wore the jersey number sixteen. As another tribute to their teammate, all the Miami Marlins players stepped into the batter's box without their typical walkup songs playing to each honor their teammate with a moment of silence. Before taking the field to start the game, Dee Gordon repeated a ritual José Fernández made routinely before each time he pitched, touching the dirt on the back of the mound before jogging to his position at second base. After a moment of silence was held in the stadium to honor José Fernández, the game began.

In the bottom in the first inning, Miami Marlins leadoff hitter Dee Gordan walked up to the plate. With tears in his eyes, Gordan, who typically bats lefty, got into to the right batter's box, wearing a #16 on his helmet and in honor of Fernández, took the first pitch. For those unfamiliar, the term "taking a pitch" actually means "not swinging" at the baseball and letting the pitch go by on purpose. Then, Gordan stepped into the left side batter's box and in honor of José, took another pitch. Then, as Mets pitcher Bartolo Colon threw the next pitch, Dee Gordon, a speedy second baseman known for stealing bases and not hitting home runs, crushed the baseball over the fence for his first home run of the season! It was a dramatic and emotional moment as Gordon crossed home plate and was greeted and embraced by his teammates. As Gordon hugged his teammates, you could clearly see that he was overcome with emotion.

The Baseball Gods made sure that the Miami Marlins defeated the New York Mets that night. Sports writer Joe Frisaro covered the clubhouse scene after the game in his MLB. com article, "After honoring friend, Dee delivers 1st homer." After the game, Dee Gordon had this to say to reporters: "It was for [Fernandez], because he loved to hit as much as he loved to pitch. I thought that was just my way of showing him that, I love you. I miss you. I'm always going to miss you." Perhaps sadly, but also amazingly, there are actually more examples of dramatic home runs in relation to death of loved ones in recent years. Take the example of Milwaukee Brewers pitcher Brandon Woodruff.

Brandon Woodruff, who also, like Bubba Derby, pitched with my former colleague Jon Perrin in 2017 with the Biloxi Shuckers, pitched the game of his life (six shut-out innings) and hit his first career home run in his first game back after his older brother Blake died in a tragic ATV accident. Then even more recently, in 2018, I watched the events unfold with Oakland A's outfielder Stephen Piscotty.

When A's outfielder Stephen Piscotty found out that his mother, Gretchen Piscotty, had ALS (Amyotrophic Lateral

Sclerosis), also known as Lou Gehrig's disease, he asked the St. Louis Cardinals to trade him to the Oakland A's so he could be closer to his mother during her last days. The St. Louis Cardinals should be commended for honoring Piscotty's trade request. Sadly, Gretchen Piscotty passed away on May 6, 2018. In Stephen's first game back after his mother's death, in his first at-bat since her funeral, he hit a home run! While all these individual examples of the holy spirit flowing through baseball players are amazing, it is even more incredible with it happens with an entire team.

On June 29, 2019, The Oakland A's defeated the Los Angeles Angels by the score of 4-0. The starting pitcher that day for the Angels was Tyler Skaggs. Just two days later, on July 1, 2019, hours before the Los Angeles Angels were scheduled to play against the Texas Rangers, Tyler Skaggs was found dead in his hotel room in Southlake, TX. The death of Skaggs was another tragic loss for the MLB community.

On July 9, 2019, Tommy La Stella and Mike Trout represented the Los Angeles Angels in Cleveland for the mid-summer classic — the All-Star Game. Trout and La Stella paid tribute to their friend and teammate and both wore Tyler Skaggs's jersey number, 45. As millions of baseball fans watched the game, behind the scenes, the Baseball Gods were preparing for perhaps the greatest Baseball Gods moment of all time.

The Los Angeles Angels held a tribute night for Tyler Skaggs on Friday, June 13, 2019. Every player on the Angels wore the jersey #45 and Skaggs on their backs. After a 45-second moment of silence, Skaggs's mother, Debbie Hetman, was introduced to throw out the ceremonial first pitch. As she approached the pitcher's mound, she wrote her son's initials,

"TY," into the dirt. Then Debbie threw a perfect strike. As she walked off the pitcher's mound, she made a prayer gesture with her hands and looked to the sky. Mrs. Hetman said after the game that she wanted to make her son proud. As Debbie threw that ceremonial first pitch, she was likely all too aware that the next day was her son's birthday.

In the bottom of the first inning, Tyler Skaggs's dear friend, Angels center fielder Mike Trout, got up to bat. Mike Trout has only swung at 16% of first pitches throughout his career. But on this night, the holy spirit was flowing through Mike Trout. Trout swung at the first pitch and crushed a home run to deep center field — the home run went 454 feet.

Standing in the outfield watching the baseball fly over his head and over the outfield wall was Dee Gordon. Yes, the same Dee Gordon that hit a home run during his first at-bat after his dear friend and former Miami Marlins teammate José Fernández passed away. You just can't make this stuff up.

Every player on the Los Angeles Angels was flowing with the holy spirit. The Angels batted around the order and Mike Trout got to bat again during the first inning. In Mike Trout's second at-bat, he hit a two-run double. Trout had four RBIs in the first inning! The score was now 10-0 and still in the bottom of the first. The holy spirit was not just flowing through the Angels' batting order, it was also felt by the pitching staff.

Starting pitcher Taylor Cole worked the first two innings and gave up no hits. Then, Angels pitcher Felix Peña came on in the third inning and proceeded to pitch seven innings without giving up a base hit — it was a combined no-hitter! After the game, the players celebrated their amazing victory and then once again paid tribute to Tyler Skaggs. One by one, each player took off his #45 jersey and placed it on the pitcher's mound.

The numerology left behind by this Baseball Gods moment is nothing short of miraculous. Recall that Tyler Skaggs was born on July 13, or 7/13. The Angels scored seven runs in the first inning and thirteen runs in the game; the last combined no-hitter thrown in the state of California was on Skaggs's actual birth date, when four Baltimore Orioles combined to shut out the Oakland Athletics on July 13, 1991. The Angels' no-hitter was the eleventh in franchise history and Skaggs wore the #11 at Santa Monica High School. Mike Trout's first inning home run was 454 ft., which is 45 forwards and backwards. The Angels finished the game facing twenty-eight batters, and Tyler Skaggs would have been twenty-eight years old.

After the game, Mike Trout said, "It was pretty incredible. He's watching over everybody and he wants everybody to do good." Angels pitcher Felix Peña said in Spanish, "This is all for him," and also said "We now have an angel protecting us from above." Angels manager Brad Ausmus said, "That was one of the most special moments I have been a part of on a major league field in 25 years...You feel like it's partly Skaggy's no-hitter." In the visiting team's locker room, sports writers were eager to get a comment from Dee Gordon, who told MLB.com, "I got one thing to say, and I said it three years ago, and I'm gonna be done with it: If you don't believe in God, you might wanna start. I said it three years ago when I hit the homer for Jose. They had a no-hitter today. Y'all better start. And that's all I got."

When I woke up the next morning, Twitter was overflowing

with posts about the Tyler Skaggs Baseball Gods moment. For me, it was most gratifying to see tweet after tweet that read "The Baseball Gods are Real!" I have a feeling that Johnny Bench, Edinson Volquez, Dee Gordon, Brandon Woodruff, Stephen Piscotty, Taylor Cole, Felix Peña and Mike Trout would all agree with me that the holy spirit and the Baseball Gods are real.

CHAPTER EIGHT

The Freak Injuries

"I feel like, looking back, if I didn't have so many injuries, who knows where my numbers could be right now.
But only God can judge me."
—Jose Reyes

WARNING: IF YOU ARE AN ACTIVE BASEBALL PLAYER AT any level, you may not want to read this chapter. Seriously, you just might want to skip it. Since many people believe that our thoughts can manifest our physical reality, I don't think it's a good idea for your mind to focus on this chapter's subject matter, not even for one second. For retired athletes and regular folks like me, I hope you find this chapter interesting and thought provoking. And on second thought, if you are an active baseball player who has been getting injured a lot recently, in strange ways, perhaps you really should read this chapter. In fact, you probably should read it very carefully.

It seems that an effective way for the Baseball Gods to get the attention of an athlete is with an injury. If a player is not getting the message, the Baseball Gods may increase the number and intensity of the injuries and, to make a point, may cause the injuries to happen in an unusual manner. When these bizarre, debilitating and painful events occur in baseball, they are called — freak injuries.

The history of freak injuries in baseball is long and well documented. Sometimes injuries happen on the ballfield. Other times, they happen elsewhere. There is a possibility that they may occur as part of an elaborate scheme built into the fabric of the universe by the Baseball Gods, possibly to help enforce the laws of karma. In this manner, they help souls living as humans on this planet to grow and evolve through adversity. When the Baseball Gods see a baseball player making poor life decisions and veering in the wrong direction on his or her spiritual path, hidden forces in the universe may intervene.

If the universe is designed to keep a person's karma in balance, an injury can be used as an effective tool to help make this happen. However, when the universe really needs to get an athlete's attention, a simple, common injury, like a mild muscle strain, might be not enough. To get a baseball player to recognize that the Baseball Gods are trying to send a serious message or a warning, the injury may need to be more severe or freakier. If the injury is sufficiently severe or freaky, it just may make the athlete more responsive and introspective.

Visualize an athlete lying in bed with a cast on his or her leg from a recent injury. Now there is time to contemplate life and revisit past actions. If the injury is serious, the athlete likely will think about what life would be like without the ability to play the sport he or she loves so much. When an athlete has something taken away, like participating in that sport, he or she may search his or her soul and decide to do whatever it takes to makes things right. Typically, after recovering from such a serious injury, an athlete becomes grateful, humbled, and yes, somehow better and stronger for having gone through and learned from the experience.

I first started thinking about the impact of a freak injury as it relates to spirituality and, more specifically, karma, after reading Zack Hample's book *The Baseball*. Hample points out that freak injuries have been happening in baseball for decades. For example, he writes that on opening day of the 1954 baseball season, Michigan Sports Hall of Fame sports writer H.G. Salsinger got hit in the face with a foul ball and lost his vision in one eye. This was freaky because Salsinger was not even on the field at the time. He was sitting in the press box. One wonders what, if anything, Salsinger may have done in the past to deserve that.

There are many other examples where an injury was considered unusual or freakish. In 1988, New York Mets first baseman Keith Hernandez broke his own nose during a batting practice session when he hit a foul ball that ricocheted off the batting cage and hit him right in the face. In 1997, Seattle Mariners relief pitcher Josias Manzanillo got hit in the groin by a Manny Ramirez line drive and needed surgery. In Game 4 of the 2001 American League Division Series, Jermaine Dye of the Oakland A's fouled a pitch off of his own leg and broke it. In 2005, Colorado Rockies outfielder Dustan Mohr jumped out of the dugout to celebrate a game-winning walk-off home run by teammate Clint Barnes and strained his groin in the process. In the same year, the same Clint Barnes fell and broke his collarbone lugging a heavy package of deer meat he got from his Rockies' teammate Todd Helton. In 2010, Marlins outfielder Chris Coghlan injured himself celebrating another game-winning hit. Coghlan went to smash a shaving cream pie into teammate Wes Helms' face, and he tore the meniscus in his left knee, needed surgery, and missed the rest of the season. In 2010, Los Angeles Angels first baseman Kendry Morales hit a game-winning tenth inning walk-off grand slam against the Seattle Mariners. When approaching home plate where his teammates were waiting for him to celebrate, Morales leaped high into the air, crashed down into the pack of players, awkwardly landed on home plate, and broke his leg. Due to the surgery and complications in rehab that followed, Morales would miss the remainder of the 2010 season and the 2011 season as well.

In his 2013 article, "The Weirdest Injuries in Baseball History," Jon Terbush gives a few additional examples of freak injuries that might demonstrate "instant karma." First, there's the tale of slugging second baseman Jeff Kent who broke his wrist in 2003 while attempting wheelies on his motorcycle. To make the matter worse, Kent initially told reporters that he was injured when he fell down while washing his car. It turns out that riding a motorcycle was specifically forbidden in his contract with his team. Did the Baseball Gods punish Kent for his reckless behavior and for lying about it? At the very least, Kent flushed millions of contract dollars down the drain as a result of this prank. Terbush also tells of Pittsburg Pirates pitcher Francisco Liriano who broke his arm on his family Christmas vacation. Initially, Liriano said his injury was the result of a fall in his bathroom. However, he actually broke his arm pounding on a door in an attempt to scare his kids. Did the Baseball Gods punish Liriano for lying? Terbush mentions outfielder Marty Cordova's mishap of falling asleep in a tanning bed and badly burning himself. Did the Baseball Gods punish Cordova for vanity? Then there's a repeat of the Clint Barnes tale where he injured his collarbone hauling deer meat. Did the Baseball Gods punish Barnes for hurting innocent animals? In some cases, the karma payback is instant. In other cases, it is not. It is simply delayed, usually for greater impact.

Although I did not know it at the time, I was personally involved in a situation which gave rise to a freak injury and karma payback. In late August 2016, my son Nate and I arrived early at Kauffman Stadium so that he could "ball-hawk" during batting practice before the Royals hosted the visiting division champion Cleveland Indians. Coincidentally, this was the same ballgame mentioned in my first book, *The Baseball Gods are Real: A True Story about Baseball and Spirituality*, during which Rajai Davis and Mike Napoli each signed a baseball for Nate. Nate and I were positioned just beyond the outfield wall when the behavior of Indians' pitcher Trevor Bauer got our attention.

By way of background, players who catch fly balls close to the outfield wall during batting practice typically toss those balls to fans in the stands. Doing so is considered good public relations, and almost all baseball players take pleasure in making young baseball fans happy. However, on this day, whenever Trevor Bauer caught a fly ball close to the outfield wall, he threw the baseball back into the infield rather than toss it to a fan. To make matters worse, Bauer would often tease and taunt the young Royals fans by pretending to toss them a ball before throwing it back toward the infield. Bauer seemed to be enjoying himself at the expense of some young, now unhappy, baseball fans.

After witnessing this behavior for about twenty minutes, some of the fathers in the stands started yelling at Bauer, "Hey, c'mon man, toss a kid a ball already!" Bauer refused to give in and after several more minutes, even I yelled out, "C'mon man, show some love, throw a kid a ball." Bauer, who seemed to enjoy taunting the fans and never did toss up even one ball, was loudly booed by the crowd when batting practice ended.

Nate walked away from that batting practice session disappointed, empty-handed and somewhat surprised by Bauer's antics. After the game and for a few days thereafter, we talked about Bauer's attitude and we wondered if the Baseball Gods would punish him for what in our view was inappropriate behavior.

While Nate and I chose to forgive Trevor Bauer for his immature, childish behavior, the Baseball Gods would not. Just a few weeks later, Bauer and the Indians were in Toronto playing Game 3 of the 2016 American League Championship Series against the Blue Jays. In the first inning, after just twenty-one pitches, Bauer had to leave the game because his lacerated finger started gushing blood. How did this happen you ask? Of course, it was the result of a freak injury discussed in detail in Andrew Daniels' *Men's Health* article, "The Dumbest Baseball Injuries of All Time." It turns out Bauer had sliced his pinky finger while playing with a flying drone a few days before the beginning of the playoffs.

Right there in Toronto, in front of a stadium full of fans and millions of people watching on television, including Nate and me, Bauer had to exit the game because the stitches on his pinky finger split apart and blood was dripping from his hand. As we watched Bauer walk off the pitcher's mound into the Indians' dugout, Nate and I looked at each other in utter amazement. We both knew Bauer's freak injury was big time karma payback, which the Baseball Gods had delayed for weeks, in a playoff situation, for maximum effect.

2017 was another year during which many ballplayers were sidelined by freak injuries. For example, Kansas City Royals left-handed relief pitcher Brian Flynn was repairing the roof on his barn in McAlester, Oklahoma during the offseason when it caved in. Flynn crashed down to the ground, was knocked out cold from the huge fall, and suffered broken ribs and non-displaced fractures in his vertebrae. Thankfully, Flynn eventually recovered from this potentially life-threatening accident, but I'm sure he wondered what he might have done to deserve it. Madison Bumgarner, a former World Series Most Valuable Player and championship pitcher with the San Francisco Giants in 2014, had never been on the injured reserve list before 2017. However, in April, just after the start of the season, Bumgarner badly strained the AC joint in his throwing shoulder when he crashed riding a dirt bike in the Colorado mountains. It took months for Bumgarner to recover from the injury and the Giants finished the season in last place. I recall seeing Bumgarner being interviewed on television, with his arm in a sling, when he told reporters, "I wish I had some kind of cool story for you that it was some kind of crazy wreck, but it really wasn't anything spectacular, just super unfortunate. I was actually being pretty safe the whole time; it was just a freak deal." A freak deal indeed. Perhaps the "freakiest" injury of 2017 goes to Texas Rangers southpaw pitcher Martin Perez. On December 11, 2017, Perez was injured by a bull on his ranch in Venezuela. Yes, you read that correctly.

When the bull made a move that startled Perez, he fell to the ground and injured the radial head in his elbow. What had Perez done to pissed off that bull? Was this freak injury karma payback? Only the Baseball Gods know for sure.

Another freakish injury occurred in 2017, close to home, so to speak, because it involved Kansas City Royals manager Ned Yost. In what was described as a "near death experience," Yost broke his pelvis and almost bled to death after falling from a deer stand on his 58-acre farm outside of Atlanta, Georgia. Kevin Spain of *USA Today* summarized the ordeal in his article "Ned Yost's Account of his Injury Shows it was More Serious than First Thought." Yost, who hunts most days during the offseason, said about the incident, "There's no doubt I would have bled out if I didn't have my cellphone with me. There was nobody that was coming. Nobody would have found me. I would have been dead by nightfall." The trauma surgeon, recalling the intense moments on the operating table during the emergency surgery, is later quoted saying to Yost, "Man, Ned, I was really scared about you. We've seen these things before – this is a 25-30 percent mortality rate. You were crashing on the table. We couldn't get the bleeding stopped. I thought we were going to lose you."

Near death experiences are well documented for being life changing catalysts. Similarly, a freak injury can dramatically change a person's life path. For example, take the case of Philadelphia Phillies pitching prospect Matt Imhof. During a resistance-training exercise session after closing out a victory for his Clearwater Threshers against the Brevard County Manatees, a metal hook broke away from the wall and smashed Imhof directly in the face. The blow to his face was so severe that his nose was broken, two orbital bones were fractured, and, worst of all, his right eye needed to be removed and replaced with a prosthetic. After two and one-half seasons in the minor leagues playing with four different teams, at the tender age of only 23, Imhof announced his retirement from baseball, the game he loved since he was a little kid. In an article he wrote for ESPN, Imhof thoughtfully explained, "I had two options. I could let this injury define me. I could be angry - no one would blame me for that. I could be depressed, feel sorry for myself and live in the past. I could let the rest of my life be defined by the worst day of my life. Or, I could pick myself up, dust myself off and move on." Turning tragedy into wisdom, and at the same time providing testimony to his character, Imhof concludes, "I am blessed that I was able to play this game for 18 years and will never forget the lessons it taught me along the way." Confirming that a freak injury can change one's life path, Imhof went on to earn a bachelor's degree, with honors, in business administration from California Polytechnic University in 2017, and is now employed as financial advisor at Focus Capital Partners servicing the firm's professional athlete clientele.

A freak injury may be the result of a random accident, karma payback, or divine intervention. Nevertheless, what may be most important is the lesson learned and the wisdom gained from such an unfortunate experience. A good example is that of Colorado Springs Sky Sox minor league infielder Mauricio Dubon. During the 2018 season, the hot-hitting Dubon had his twenty-three-game hitting streak put on hold when he was injured during a rundown between first and second base and blew out his knee. The injury required

surgery and ended Dubon's season. While perhaps not techni-
cally a "freak injury," serious damage rarely occurs during a
rundown. Maybe a sprained ankle, but rarely an injury requir-
ing surgical repair. However, Dubon, like pitcher Matt Imhoff,
took a positive approach in dealing with this career setback.
Dubon tweeted, "Everything happens for a reason just gotta
trust God's plan til 2019 brew crew be ready the lion still alive
#blessed." The power of positive thinking must have worked
because in 2019, after rehabilitating his knee back to health,
Dubon was traded from the Milwaukee Brewers to the San
Francisco Giants. Shortly after the trade, Dubon's life-long
dream came true. He was called up from the Giant's Triple-
AAA squad to their major league roster. For the first time in
his career, Dubon had finally made it to "The Show."

Instant karma freak injuries continued in 2018. On May 15,
Red Sox relief pitcher Carson Smith gave up a home run to
Oakland A's slugger Khris Davis. Smith was taken out of the
game, entered the dugout in a fist full of rage, and, in frustra-
tion, slammed his baseball glove down as hard as he could. By
doing so, Smith suffered a right shoulder subluxation, which
ended his season. Earlier in the same year, another freak injury
occurred, this time to former American League Cy Young
Award winner Blake Snell. After a shower, Snell tried to move
a decorative granite stand in his bathroom, didn't realize that
the stand had three parts, and one part fell on his right foot
badly smashing a toe. While Blake Snell's odd injury happened
in the bathroom, Pitcher Shawn Kelley's freak injury, when
he was with the Oakland A's, occurred in the kitchen. Kelley
accidentally sliced the tip of his right thumb on a sharp knife
while washing the dishes. Salvador Perez' freak injury also

happened at home. The Kansas City Royals' all-star catcher and 2015 World Series MVP tore the medial collateral ligament in his left knee while carrying heavy luggage up a flight of stairs at home just before the start of the 2018 season. The lessons learned by baseball players: don't give up a home run and slam your glove down, don't put a granite stand in your bathroom and try to move it, don't wash sharp knives, and don't lift heavy luggage up a staircase.

Two years later, during the first week of 2020, the New York sports pages reported another very freakish injury. New York Mets outfielder Yoenis Cespedes' suffered multiple fractures in his right ankle as a result of a violent fall at his Port St. Lucie ranch caused by a wild boar that charged him after escaping from a trap. Yes, this is the same Mr. Cespedes who strained his left hamstring in 2017 causing manager Terry Collins to place blame on the Baseball Gods.

To be fair and balanced, I realize that accidents do happen, often a result of bad luck or coincidence. Nor am I suggesting that every time a ballplayer gets injured, it's because the Baseball Gods are dishing out punishment for some karmic wrongdoing or misdeed. However, many managers, coaches, players and sports writers will tell you with a straight face that there is some kind of invisible, intelligent energy that permeates all things in baseball. It is nowhere and yet it is everywhere. It is like an invisible umpire that is always at work, calling balls, strikes and outs in the game of life. It never takes a day off and is constantly balancing thoughts, choices, actions and consequences. My thesis, freak injuries may be fingerprints left behind by the Baseball Gods.

CHAPTER NINE

The Lessons of Baseball Karma

"Right now, somebody has pissed off the baseball gods, because every move we make has been the wrong one."
—Terry Collins

A TAKEAWAY FROM THE PREVIOUS CHAPTER IS THAT A freak injury may be accidental or just the result of bad luck. Another takeaway may be that to increase the probability of avoiding a freak injury, it may be wise for a baseball player, and frankly all humans, to create good karma.

For those unfamiliar with the concept of karma, it is a belief system at the core of several world religions including Hinduism, Buddhism, Ayyavazhi, Sikhism, and Jainism. The law of karma states that the sum of a person's actions in this and previous states of existence determine his or her fate and future existences. In terms of spiritual development, karma encompasses all that a person has done, is doing, and will do. Karma is not about punishment or reward. It is energy created every time a person is kind to another being. However, it is also energy created whenever a person causes suffering or harm to another being. Individuals can create good karma by being honest and telling the truth, by helping others, by being kind and compassionate, by thinking positive thoughts, by doing yoga, by eating healthy, and by living a purposeful life. You can guess, I'm sure, how bad karma is created.

In his article "Is There Such a Thing as Baseball Karma?" published in the *Bleacher Report* on August 11, 2008, Sports writer Brad Finn, a die-hard fan of the Boston Red Sox, celebrates the injuries of players on the first-place Tampa Bay Rays. Finn writes with delight, "As I write this, Carl Crawford and Evan Longoria, both of the Tampa Bay Rays, have landed on the disabled list, Crawford with a hand injury and Longoria with a wrist injury. I am not too broken up about this news. In fact, I am fairly gleeful about it." Finn believes the Red Sox appear to be incapable of winning the division on their own merits, so he wishes for bad things to happen to other teams, in this case specifically, injuries to the players of the rival, the first-place Rays. Finn knows that he is baiting the Baseball Gods writing, "Am I tempting the fates by taking pleasure in the pain of others? Is it possible that such selfish behavior will bring the wrath of the Karma gods down upon the Red Sox?" In his conclusion, Finn decides it is worth the risk and says, "So bring it, Karma!" Coincidence or not, the Red Sox did not make it to the World Series that year, the Rays did. Red Sox fans would have to wait another decade before their team won their next World Series. I should also point out that the Baseball Gods appear to have a sense of humor. The year after Finn wrote his baseball karma article, the New York Yankees, the most hated rival of the Boston Red Sox, went on to win the World Series.

Karma may have had an impact on some of the great-est baseball players to ever play the game. In 2016, all-time home run hitting record-setter Barry Bonds and seven-time Cy Young Award-winning strike-out legend Roger Clemens were eligible to be nominated into the National Baseball Hall of Fame. Also, on this list of potential inductees that year were the home run hitting duo of Mark McGwire and Sammy Sosa. Under ordinary circumstances, players with their accomplish-ments and statistics would be shoe-ins for acceptance into the Hall. However, all four players were rejected. The reason? They all cheated the game of baseball by taking steroids, ille-gal performance enhancing drugs, and the members of the Baseball Writers Association of America, who vote to select inductees, were unforgiving.

A close look at the effect steroids can have on a baseball player's performance is obvious. In 1998, McGwire hit 70 home runs at the age of 34. The next year, he hit 65 home runs. Yet in the years 1986 through 1995 as a much younger man, he reached a season high of 49 home runs only once. In 2001, Bonds, at the age of 36, hit 73 home runs, the most he or anyone else ever hit in one season. Prior to that year, Bonds had never hit 50 home runs in a single season. In 2005, Clemens posted an ERA of 1.87 and logged 211 innings at the age of 42. That was his lowest ERA ever, even lower than his ERA in each of his 7 Cy Young seasons. During this period of time, many players were taking steroids to improve their on-field perfor-mance and many got caught. Baseball fans and sports writers for years were questioning whether the ball was juiced or was it the players. It became clear that it was the players, and the years associated with their unbelievably incredible statistical achievements became known as the "steroids era."

According to the insightful January 7, 2016 editorial in the *Amarillo Globe-News*, "Baseball Karma Strikes Back," karma is credited as the reason that Bonds, Clemens, McGwire and Sosa are not in the Hall of Fame. Quoting the editorial, "And consider this: Clemens and Bonds have not played since 2007, McGwire since 2001. We are approaching almost a decade since this trio left the game, and today's power hitters are not within striking distance of Bonds and his 73 homers in a single season in 2001. The closest in 58. So we are to assume that Bonds, at the age of 36, was better than every other power hitting that has come along since, some much younger than he was in 2001? We are not buying it - and neither should those who vote and determine the players that have earned the honor of being enshrined in Cooperstown." Karma is always at work, both good and bad. The Baseball Gods seem to be keenly aware of the improper and harmful things people do, like cheating in baseball. And because of that, a price is paid.

Karma and the Baseball Gods seem to keep track of little things too. Take, for example, the interaction in 2016 between Los Angeles Angels centerfielder Mike Trout and Houston Astros second baseman Jose Altuve, two of baseball's very best players. Altuve got a base hit and was running so fast rounding first base on his way to second that his helmet came off his head. The helmet hit Altuve on the back of his heel causing him to stumbled and then fall on his face in the dirt on the base path. The embarrassing fall, a very awkward moment for the usually fleet-footed Altuve, was seen by all, including Trout from his position in the outfield.

The next day warming up on the field before the game, Trout spent some time talking with Altuve and teased him about his base-running blunder the day before. Then, during the game,

Trout got an extra-base hit and while touching second on his way to third, right in front of where Altuve was standing, he tripped over the bag and embarrassingly fell flat on his stomach. Trout got up, managed to get back safely to second base, dusted himself off with a smile on his face, and immediately said something to Altuve that put a smile on his face. Maybe Trout and Altuve were smiling because they knew that Trout had just experienced karma payback. Or perhaps both realized, after experiencing similar embarrassing moments a day apart, that they just had a close encounter with the Baseball Gods.

Sports writer Michael Cerami tells of this incident in his 2016 interesting and humorous article "Baseball Karma Bites Mike Trout After He Gave Jose Altuve a Hard Time." Cerami comments, "Little did Trout know, the universe heard what he said to Altuve and had something planned for him, as well." I think Mike Trout knows it now, and is not likely to forget it any time soon.

Sports writers were eager to learn more about what was said between Trout and Altuve. Adrian Garro, in his MLB.com article "Kindred Spirits Mike Trout and Jose Altuve Bonded After Trout Took a Tumble Around Second Base," repeats some great quotes from both players. Altuve, talking to MLB.com's Brian McTaggart about the moment, said, "When we were stretching before the game, he [Trout] was like, 'What are you doing? You don't know how to run the bases?' And then after he fell down, he looked straight at me and said, 'My bad, I'm sorry.'" Trout, confirming the pregame conversation with MLB.com's Alden Gonzalez, said "There's kind of some karma involved. I was messing with him before the game, and

I just fell. I was laughing. It was just a funny moment. We're just out there having fun. Obviously, you're not trying to trip. But it just happened. He just fell. That's why I went to him. I told him, 'Man, I shouldn't have messed with you.' It was funny." Clearly, Mike Trout, the best centerfielder in baseball, believes in baseball karma.

While some players like Mike Trout are learning the value of avoiding bad karma, other ballplayers seem to already know the benefits of creating good karma. Perhaps that is the reason so many professional athletes support charitable organizations and volunteer to help programs designed to help kids find their way on the life's path.

Let's explore the mystery of good karma and the success achieved by ballplayers on the Washington Nationals who volunteered their time at the Celebrity Baseball Camp held every summer at Georgetown University in the nation's capital. After volunteering at the camp in the morning, Nationals shortstop Trea Turner went five-for-five with a walk that afternoon. Wilson Ramos, the former Nationals catcher now with the New York Mets, had two career games, each time after he volunteered at the camp. Outfielder Roger Bernadina went 3-for-3 at the plate and made a SportsCenter Top 10 catch the night after he volunteered at the camp. Nationals rookie pitcher Taylor Jordan got his first career win in the major leagues after attending the camp. Ian Desmond went on one of the best hitting streaks of his career, going nine for fifteen in the next four games, after attending the camp. Nationals third baseman Anthony Rendon visited the camp on his day off and hit a home run the very next day. Perhaps the best good karma performance in the camp's long list of miraculous achievements goes to Max Scherzer, who pitched the first no-hitter of his career on June 20, 2015, just three hours after volunteering at the camp. All these and additional positive events are documented in Hal Jalikakik's excellent article "Does Good Karma Lead to Career Performances in Baseball? Jalikakik investigated this question and the answer seems clear. It does.

In addition to supporting charitable causes and volunteering to help kids, there are other ways to create good karma. One way is to be a genuinely good, decent human being who does the right thing. Another way is to be honest and unselfish. For example, in 2015, Chicago Cubs shortstop Starlin Castro was having a break-out season and was selected to the National League All-Star team. Talking to reporters about Castro making yet another great defensive play, Cubs manager Joe Maddon said, "Everything he's doing right now, I always believe in the complimentary effects of everything that we do. And if there's good baseball karma, he's created that for himself right now by the way he's gone about that business."

Maddon witnessed another good baseball karma moment in 2019 related to utility player and two-time World Series champion Ben Zobrist. Early in the season, the manager was trying something new and radical by issuing his starting lineups three days in advance. Veteran Zobrist, in a slump batting only .239 at the time, knew he was scheduled to be in the starting lineup the next day. Zobrist also knew that the night before, his teammate David Bote had hit two home runs. Given these circumstances, Zobrist went into his manager's office and suggested to Maddon that he play Bote the next night instead of him. It was a selfless move on Zobrist's part, and he later told the

Chicago Sun Times, "Frankly, there was a little tension in my competitive heart, but it was the right thing to do." Maddon took Zobrist's advice and started Bote, who delivered with a double and played solid defensively at both second and third base. Late in the extra-inning game, Maddon substituted in Zobrist who reached base in each of his three plate appearances, including a two-run double in the fifteenth inning. Later in that inning, Zobrist scored the winning run on a sacrifice fly. To top off the good karma, it was a diving catch by, yes indeed, Ben Zobrist at the left field wall to secure the final out of the game, with the tying run on base. The Cubs defeated the Arizona Diamondbacks 6-5 that night, a ballgame filled with Baseball Gods moments, retold by Nick Vlahos in his *Peoria Journal Star* article "Excellent Karma for Ben Zobrist in Cubs' Marathon Victory."

Based on their actions and the consequences that followed, I'm fairly certain that Barry Bonds, Roger Clemens, Mark McGuire, Sammy Sosa, Mike Trout, Max Scherzer, and Ben Zobrist all believe that baseball karma is real.

CHAPTER TEN

The Superstitions

"I have just one superstition. Whenever I hit a homerun, I make
certain I touch all four bases."
—Babe Ruth

I REMEMBER A WARM, BREEZY EVENING IN BILOXI,
Mississippi, casually walking from my hotel to dinner with
then minor league pitcher Jon Perrin, my friend and former
apprentice and colleague at Satya Investment Management,
when I asked if he was superstitious. I had flown down to
Biloxi from Kansas City earlier that day because I wanted to
see Perrin pitch in a baseball game in person for the first time.
Perrin admitted that he did have the same pre-game routine
every day but did not consider himself to be superstitious. In
fact, Perrin said that he tried to avoid superstitions because he
believed that a baseball player can become a slave to them. I
recall that conversation so well because of events that trans-
pired over several days during the next baseball season.

Perrin, after pitching for years at all levels in the minor
league system with several different teams, happily received
an invitation from the Milwaukee Brewers organization

to attend their major league spring training program in the Cactus League in Arizona. Since I was eager and anxious to see Perrin's professional pitching debut, off I went to Phoenix. During my visit, Perrin told me that a custom baseball cleat company contacted him and asked if he would design and customize his own Nike branded cleats. Perrin loved the idea. Given his interest in finance and investments, he chose a "stock market" theme that displayed actual stock charts of a rising bull market on the sides of the cleats. The charts were so detailed that they even included bar charts.

Months later on May 25, 2018, long after I returned to Kansas City with a portfolio of great spring training stories to fill several chapters of my next baseball book, Perrin's custom stock market cleats arrived in the mail. He texted me a photo of the cleats, which I thought looked awesome and just might bring him some good luck. Into Perrin's travel bag they went, just in time for him, now back in the minor leagues with the Colorado Springs Sky Sox, to take them on a road trip to Tennessee for a series against the Memphis Red Birds. Three days later, in the last game of the Red Birds series, Perrin came in as a relief pitcher wearing his custom-made cleats. He pitched well in his one inning of work and did not give up any runs. After the game, I texted Perrin to say that his new cleats were working and brought him good luck.

Perrin and his Sky Sox teammates returned home after their Memphis road trip to host the visiting Iowa Cubs. Perrin pitched twice in this series, on May 31 and then again on June 1. In 2.2 innings in those two home games, Perrin did not give up any hits and his stock market cleats now had a three-game scoreless streak.

Less than a week later, Perrin travelled to the West Coast for the first time. The Sky Sox road trip to California included a series in Fresno and another in Sacramento. On June 7, when Perrin emerged from the bullpen to take the mound, I was surprised to see that he was not wearing his stock market cleats. I thought, "What is he doing? Those cleats have a three-game scoreless streak going." In his one inning of work against Fresno that night, Perrin gave up two hits and two unearned runs. To make matters worse, one of the hits was a home run.

Texting with Perrin after the game, I urged him to wear the custom cleats the next time he pitched, and he did. On June 11 in Sacramento, I was pleased to see the good luck cleats back where I thought they belonged, on Perrin's feet, not on the floor of his locker. Perrin faced only one batter in relief that night, got him out, and the stock market cleats began a new scoreless streak. Perrin wore the cleats again on June 14, 15 and 17, and did not give up any runs during those three outings.

Despite his current hot streak, the Brewers organization demoted Perrin from the AAA Colorado Springs Sky Sox to the AA Biloxi Shuckers. A few days later on June 22, Perrin wore the stock market cleats in his first outing with his new team and again pitched well. Now, Perrin and his special cleats had five scoreless appearances in a row and a total of eight consecutive appearances without giving up an earned run.

Again, to my surprise, Perrin decided not wear the stock market cleats on June 26, when the Biloxi Shuckers played on the road against Charlotte Knights, an affiliate of the Chicago White Sox. Perrin pitched two innings and gave up three hits and one earned run. After returning home from the road trip,

Perrin wore the cleats again on June 30 against the Mobile Bay Bears, and the scoreless streak was extended to nine games. It seemed simply uncanny to me. I began to wonder if Perrin was intentionally switching on and off to avoid becoming superstitious about these custom cleats. He chose to not wear them on July 5 against the Braves in Jackson, Mississippi, pitched three strong innings, but did give up one earned run.

On July 9, playing at home against the visiting Jacksonville Jumbo Shrimp, the stock market cleats were finally challenged and their good luck streak was truly in jeopardy. Perrin's stat line was impressive, 2.0 innings, 2 hits, 0 earned runs, 0 walks and 3 strike outs, but box scores can be deceiving. Perrin was in peril on the pitcher's mound late in the game. With two outs and runners on first and third, the batter crushed a Perrin fastball to deep left field. It had home run written all over it. However, speedy left fielder Troy Stokes Jr. tracked the ball perfectly and made an amazing diving catch on the warning track right in front of the outfield wall. The scoreless streak was still intact.

But few things go on forever, including the good luck generated by special cleats. Perrin finally gave up an earned run wearing them on July 12 during a road game against the Jumbo Shrimp in Jacksonville. I wonder if this impressive 10 game scoreless streak changed Perrin's view on superstitions. I doubt it.

When it comes to baseball players and superstitions, the stories are legion. You could fill several shelves at your local Barnes and Noble or neighborhood library with books on this subject alone. As these books will attest, ballplayers can be superstitious about rituals that they perform before, during and after a game. They can be superstitious about things they wear, things they eat, and things they say, read or pray on game day. Interestingly, they can even become superstitious about personal hygiene.

Noah Syndergaard and Jacob DeGrom, the dynamic pitching duo for the New York Mets, were taking the National League by storm in 2016. They had more than nasty fastballs in common. They both maintained very long, shoulder-length blond hair for good luck. Syndergaard's was so long that he earned the nickname "Thor" because of his resemblance to the Marvel superhero who also had long, flowing golden locks. When asked by sportswriter Lindy Segal why he kept his hair so long, DeGrom said, "When I used to cut it in the minor leagues, I felt I gave up runs afterwards, so I quit cutting it." This interview is highlighted in Segal's *People* magazine article "We're in a Golden Age of Baseball Hair: 4 Reasons Long Locks are Back in Style on the Field."

In addition to the many individual baseball players that are superstitious, sometimes this phenomenon carries over to a team level. Take, for example, the 2016 Kansas City Royals. Following their epic 2014 and 2015 seasons, when they won back-to-back American League championships and a World Series, the team began to struggle during the 2016 season after losing some key players to free agency. By mid-season, the team was looking for a spark to get them on a winning streak. That's when the team received a small gift from the Baseball Gods.

On a typically hot, humid August night at Kauffman Stadium, a large green praying mantis flew into the Royals dugout. As the game progressed, this flying insect stayed in the dugout and appeared to be watching the game. The Royals went on to win the game and declared that the praying mantis had brought them good luck. The team gave the bug the nickname "Rally Mantis" and made it their new team mascot. Royals outfielder Billy Burnes was designated the guardian of Rally Mantis and he built a cage for the insect so the team could take it on their upcoming road trip. Pitcher Ian Kennedy became the "travel caretaker" responsible for carrying the praying mantis and its cage.

Unfortunately, after winning two series in a row, Rally Mantis died on the team's road trip to Minnesota. The players paid their respects and even made a tribute video to honor the passing of their mascot. Nevertheless, the team was superstitious about the power of the insect and believed it brought them good luck. The Royals went 5-1 in the six games the team and Rally Mantis were together.

As fate, or the Baseball Gods, would have it, another green praying mantis flew into the team's visiting dugout in Detroit, the next stop on their road trip. It was as if the Rally Mantis had been reincarnated and volunteered to become the team's next mascot. The Royals swept that series against the Tigers and now had won eight out of nine games with the help of the second Rally Mantis. However, knowing what had happened to the first Rally Mantis, the players decided to set the insect free.

Baseball superstitions are by no means limited to wearing apparel like special cleats or team mascots like the Rally Mantis. Some ballplayers believe even a secret salsa recipe can bring them good luck. Take, for example, what happened to St. Louis Cardinals veteran infielder Matt Carpenter, with the assistance of pitcher Adam Wainwright, his good friend and teammate.

During the 2018 season, Carpenter was in the worst batting slump of his career. Wainwright, an avid gardener, had an unusual idea to help Carpenter bust out of his slump.

He planted a variety of fruits and vegetables in Carpenter's back yard without his knowledge. Carpenter returned from a road trip to see Wainwright's handiwork. Part of his back yard had been turned into a garden. When it was time for a mini harvest, Carpenter decided to make homemade salsa using his recently-planted, garden-fresh fruits and vegetables.

Carpenter's homemade salsa must have been tasty because one day he decided to bring some to the Cardinal's clubhouse. This is where the story really gets interesting. That day Carpenter hit a home run against the visiting Cincinnati Reds. The next day he brought the salsa to the ballpark again and, you guessed it, he hit another home run against the Reds. With a consecutive game home run streak going, Carpenter decided to bring the salsa with him on the Cardinal's road trip to Chicago to play a 4-game weekend series against the Cubs at Wrigley Field. On Friday night, Carpenter hit another home run. On Saturday, Carpenter went 5-for-5, hit 3 more home runs, and 2 doubles to boot. Now he had hit six home runs during a four-game home run streak. Then on Sunday, to the dismay of loyal Cubs fans, Carpenter hit home runs in both games of a double-header. To the delight of his fans back home in St. Louis, and no doubt to the delight of the Baseball Gods as well, Carpenter's home run hot streak tied him with Mark McGwire's franchise record for consecutive games with a home run.

After the second game of the double-header, Carpenter said of his recent surge in home runs, "Maybe it's the salsa." Not about to change his newfound good luck, Carpenter continued, "I don't know. But I'm going to keep eating it for sure." It wasn't just Carpenter who became superstitious about the special salsa. The St. Louis Cardinals mentioned the miraculous consecutive home run hitting streak on Twitter with this message: "When you have a day like @MattCarp13 had yesterday you keep everything in your pre-game routine the exact same... right down to the homemade salsa!"

When it comes to superstitions in baseball, I think the 2016 Kansas City Royals, Adam Wainwright and Matt Carpenter would agree they exist and can have an impact on performance. Perhaps Jon Perrin might agree as well. In any case, I'm sure they all agree that the Baseball Gods are Real!

CHAPTER ELEVEN

The Rituals

"I like to take four warm-up swings in the on-deck circle.
Not five, not three."
—Mike Lowell

THE GAME OF BASEBALL IS FILLED WITH MANY DIFFER-
ent kinds of rituals. There's the playing of the National
Anthem before the beginning of the game, the ceremonial first
pitch, the home plate umpire screaming "play ball," the 7th
inning stretch, rally caps, red, white and blue banners laced
around the upper deck on opening day, just to highlight a
few. Even ballpark food and snacks are ritualistic, right down
to drinking soda and beer and eating hot dogs, peanuts and
crackerjacks.

Just like organized religions, baseball is filled with tradition, ceremony and ritualistic behavior. While fans certainly
have their rituals, baseball players are notorious for them.
Many ballplayers are so dedicated to their rituals that a
professional psychiatrist might even diagnose some of them as
having obsessive-compulsive disorder. Here are a few examples which you may find amusing.

Retired third baseman Wade Boggs, who played most of his outstanding Hall of Fame career with the Boston Red Sox, was well-known for eating chicken before every game. He also fielded exactly 150 groundballs during his pre-game routine, which may explain why he was awarded two Golden Gloves during his career. Former Minnesota Twins pitcher Ervin Santana sniffed baseballs before he threw them while home run hitter Edwin Encarnacion sniffed his baseball bat when he came to the plate. Relief pitcher Turk Wendell chewed four pieces of black licorice each inning he pitched. Wendell would spit out the licorice after each inning, then brush his teeth in the dugout, and repeat the ritual again in the next inning. Outfielder Yasiel Puig licks his baseball bat in between pitches. Alex Bregman, third baseman for the Houston Astros, once shaved his face in between innings during a game against the Kansas City Royals hoping it would help him break out of a batting slump. Also, during the 2019 World Series, Bregman started a pregame ritual of wearing the same red flannel shirt and dark blue pants to the ballpark every day. Maybe that's why he hit a grand slam in Game 4 of the series.

While Bregman did wear the same clothes before each game of the World Series, his ritual was not nearly as unsanitary as some others. For example, and hard for me to believe as I researched this subject, Moises Alou became notorious for urinating on his hands for good luck. He also thought it helped him grip the bat better. Other players, including Yankee catcher Jorge Posada, admitted to following in Alou's footsteps. Outfielder Tori Hunter once admitted that if he got three hits in a game, he would wear the same dirty underwear in the following game. Detroit Tigers manager Jim Leyland admitted that he too would not change his underwear during a team winning streak.

Common sense would have you believe that none of these rituals should bring a baseball player or manager success. However, there may be more going on here than meets the eye at first glance. Remember, a baseball ritual does not need to be spiritual in nature and may actually help a ballplayer calm his mind and relax. A player who is calm and content will likely become more confident, perhaps even get into "the zone" and have more success. Rituals help many players feel like they have more control over their destiny. In any case, professional athletes who implement rituals and follow them religiously believe they are being well-served by doing so.

While the ritualistic behavior of baseball players may be superstitious in nature, its benefits may be supported by science. Let's look at the work of psychologist B.F. Skinner, who taught pigeons how to play ping pong. Skinner, a well-known and respected twentieth-century psychologist, hypothesized that behavior was caused only by external factors, not by thoughts or emotions. In his experiments, he observed how quickly pigeons learned to associate behavior with rewards or punishment, just as humans do. Skinner's conclusion, when applied to baseball, would indicate that there is a casual connection between the ritual and a successful outcome. Thus, if a baseball player performs a ritual like kissing his bat as he enters the batter's box and gets a hit, he will link the ritualistic behavior with the base hit. If the batter does the same ritual again the next time at bat and gets another hit, the ritualistic behavior may become more habitual, and may even become associated with "good luck." In this manner, an action that began as a ritual, followed by successful results, can become a superstition.

Rituals seem to me to be rather harmless and may even have some tangible benefits. However, there may also be a dark side to ritualistic behavior. During my research on this subject, I learned about a psychological phenomenon called "the gambler's fallacy," a mistaken connection between the past and the future performance of large random events. According to this theory, when a ritual fails to produce the desired result after some initial success, a gambler will continue to delude himself with rationalizations.

Similarly, sometimes baseball players come full circle with respect to rituals and superstitions. For example, retired Red Sox pitcher Ryan Dempster told the Associated Press in 2012, "I was more superstitious when I was younger. I used to always eat a grilled chicken sandwich before every start from like '98 to 2002 maybe. I stopped when I realized it wasn't the chicken sandwich affecting my success." Dempsey is just one of many ballplayers who have come full circle on this type of behavior.

For those who believe baseball rituals are bogus, let's revisit the Yan Gomes story described in Chapter Four. You may recall that the Cleveland Indians catcher was in a terrible batting slump during the 2016 season. The team held a ceremony in their clubhouse and performed a ritual sacrifice of a chicken to the voodoo doll Jobu on behalf of Gomes. Did the ritual ceremony work? I do not know for sure, but some good things did happen for Gomez and his teammates thereafter. Cleveland went on to win the American League championship and made it to the World Series. Then, the Indians made it to the playoffs again the next season.

As for Gomes and his teammates, after trailing the New York Yankees by a score of 8 to 3 in Game 2 of the American League Division Series, the Indians made an epic comeback to tie the score at eight. In the eleventh inning, Gomes made a terrific pick-off throw to preserve the tie. Then, to complete the stunning comeback, the Indians ultimately won the game with a dramatic walk-off base hit in the bottom of the thirteenth inning. There was a runner on second base, no outs, and a three-and-two count on the batter. The batter smashed a base hit down the third baseline to win the game. The home team crowd went crazy. The man at the plate for the game-winning, extra inning hit was, you guessed it — Yan Gomes.

I think that Wade Boggs, Ervin Santana, Yasiel Puig, Edwin Encarnacion, Moises Alou, Jorge Posada, Turk Wendell, Tori Hunter, Jim Leyland and Yan Gomes would agree that rituals and baseball are joined at the hip, and that the Baseball Gods are Real.

CHAPTER TWELVE

The Zealots

"I'm actually having a positive influence on strangers' lives, and I feel like I'm making a difference."
— Laurence Leavy, "The Marlins Man"

WITHIN RELIGIOUS COMMUNITIES, MANY MEMBERS HAVE a casual interest and participate only on particular dates or special occasions. That might be Easter Sunday and Christmas Eve for Christians or Passover and Yom Kippur for Jews. On the other hand, some members are extremely dedicated and rarely miss a religious service. They attend church every Sunday or go to synagogue every Friday night and Saturday morning. Then there are a few individuals who take their religious observation to the extreme. They are perceived as "religious fanatics," given their unrelenting enthusiasm and passion for their religion, which borders on obsession.

The game of baseball has its own brand of fanatics known as "die-hard" fans. These extremely dedicated baseball loyalists truly love the game, follow the sport closely, and root for their team as enthusiastically and passionately, with as much dedication, as any religious zealot. As a long-time baseball fan, a participant since childhood, and someone who loves the game so much to have written several books about baseball, I consider myself a "die-hard."

With respect to die-hards, I loved the story of an Atlanta Braves fan named "Caitliñ" who made a bet with the Baseball Gods on Twitter during the 2018 National League Division Playoff Series. In the second inning of the game between the Atlanta Braves and the Los Angeles Dodgers, Caitlin posted "If Acuña slams this I will tattoo his face on my forearm NO LIE." The post went viral. And the Baseball Gods answered her prayers. The Braves rookie outfielder did indeed hit a home run and it was a grand slam. Caitlin did not disappoint. She got the tattoo.

While some die-hard fans like Caitlin are willing to sacrifice their flesh, others are willing to sacrifice their time and energy. That was the case with a fanatical baseball fan named Donna who earned a popular nickname, the "Stretch Lady." Donna became somewhat famous in the baseball community in 2017 when MLB.com ran a story that told the tale of her devotion to her hometown team and her attempt to help them win ball-games. For an amazing period of twelve straight years, this extremely loyal Baltimore Orioles fan sat right above the visiting team's bullpen. As soon as a relief pitcher on the opposing team got up from the bench in the bullpen and started to warm up, Donna would mimic every single thing that player did. By doing this, the "Stretch Lady" was basically trolling the opposing team's pitchers and silently heckling them. Donna became quite skilled at impersonation and she was able to success-fully mimic every stretch position and pitching motion of the opposing team's pitchers. As the ballplayers and coaches in the bullpen noticed what "Stretch Lady Donna" was doing, they started to laugh, got distracted, and lost focus. This was particularly evident the night the MLB reporters attended Camden Yards to do their story about the Stretch Lady. That evening, when Pirates relief pitcher Tony Watson got up to warm up, Donna did her thing. She mimicked his every move and apparently got into his head. Watson came into the game and proceeded to give up a pinch hit, two-run home run in the bottom of the ninth inning to give the Orioles the win. The Baseball Gods must have been laughing their butts off that night.

On the subject of funny stories about baseball fanatics, my hometown Kansas City Royals have a few of their own. During the 2014 season, two die-hard Royals fans attended every game wearing skin-tight, full body onesie outfits that featured a giant picture of a cat on the front. These guys became known as the "Cat Suit Guys" and were deemed unofficial mascots of the team. Their positive energy vibration was felt by the hometown fans and by the Royals players as well. At one Royals game I attended late in the season, the contribution of the "Cat Suit Guys" was recognized. They received an award for their fan loyalty, passion and relentless enthusiasm.

As a result of their antics, articles about the "Cat Suit Guys" began to surface. One of the guys, John Stoner, is a consultant who happens to be a die-hard Kansas City Chiefs football fan as well. Stoner's cat-suit partner, Paul Long, is a motivational speaker and author who I became friendly with years later through a mutual friend. Game after game in 2014 and 2015, Stoner and Long were visible at Kauffman Stadium holding up signs and leading Royals fans in cheers and chants. Maybe the "Cat Suit Guys" helped the Royals make it to the World Series in 2014 and again in 2015, the year the team won the championship. Only the Baseball Gods know for sure.

Another Kansas City Royals fanatic often seen at Kauffman Stadium is an elderly man with a white beard, dressed head to toe in a red, white, and blue superhero outfit. He may appear old, but he is in great shape. He runs back and forth and up and down all around the stadium throughout the games motivating the fans to get excited and cheer for the Royals. As a die-hard, I am certain that this fellow believes running around the K as he does is the perfect way to spend a day at the ballpark.

In addition to guys dressed in cat suits and an old guy wearing a colorful superhero outfit, the Kansas City Royals have an official mascot. More than two decades ago, on April 5, 1996, Sluggerrr, the now famous and loveable lion who wears a crown, became the official mascot of the Royals. Sluggerrr has entertained millions of baseball fans at the K and across the country on television.

In addition to Sluggerrr, beginning in 2014, a new, unofficial mascot found a home at Kauffman Stadium. It's not a lion with a crown or a cat in a onesie. It's a giant bird. A baseball zealot who took the name Victor Redtail has been attending almost every Royals home game for the last six years. Redtail truly believes that his presence at these ballgames brings the team good luck. He also believes that his presence makes the young fans happy, especially when he graciously takes a photo with them. I took a photo with Redtail last year and gave him a signed copy of my first book, *The Baseball Gods are Real*, as a thank you. I was happy for the photo and Redtail seemed equally happy to receive the signed copy of my book.

Toward the latter part of the 2018 season, during the National League Division Playoff Series between the Colorado Rockies and the Milwaukee Brewers, I was in the lovely city of Milwaukee on a multi-city book tour. Attending a game at Miller Park, I had the opportunity to actually meet another baseball fanatic who has become one of the most recognizable and famous figures all across the sports world — the Marlins Man. I gave the Marlins Man a signed copy of my first Baseball Gods book and when I ran into him years later at Arrowhead Stadium during the 2019 AFC Championship game, he told me he read it!

The Marlins Man, whose real name is Laurence Leavy, is a true die-hard sports fan who began gaining fame in 2012 for his frequent appearances at major sporting events wearing bright orange Miami Marlins apparel. I first learned about the Marlins Man two years later during the 2014 World Series. I remember it well. The Royals, after a very successful season and playoff run, made it to their first World Series in thirty years. Each night of the series played at Kauffman Stadium, the seats were filled with loyal Royals fans, all dressed in the team's color, royal blue. There was one exception. Sitting in the stands right behind home plate was a guy wearing a bright orange Miami Marlins baseball jersey. I wondered who this brave person was and how did he get that ticket right behind the catcher. It turns out that the person who got my attention was the Marlins Man. He got the attention of others as well, including David Glass, the owner of the Kansas City Royals at the time.

According to the tale as told by the Marlins Man, Mr. Glass was not happy to see a bright orange Marlins jersey amongst a sea of royal blue in the stands behind home plate and on television. Mr. Glass contacted the Marlins Man, through an employee of the Royals speaking on his behalf, and offered him a box suite on the second level of the stadium so he would not be seen behind the plate or on TV during Game 2 of the series. The Marlins Man declined this generous offer saying that he preferred to watch the games up close. He also said that he had worn the same jersey and sat in similar locations at previous playoff games in Baltimore and San Francisco. However, he did not stand out in the crowd at those games because the team color of both franchises is orange. Later that day, Leavy told *Miami Herald* reporters that he planned to attend the next game at Kauffman Stadium and would again be wearing his favorite orange Miami Marlins jersey, sitting in the same location.

This story gained traction and during this process I acquired quite a bit more information about the Marlins Man and why he was such a die-hard sports fan. I learned the reason that he felt so strongly about sitting in his favorite front row seat behind the catcher, a ritual at every baseball game he attends. I also gained a keen appreciation why he was unwilling to move his seat for Game 2, despite receiving the offer of a "better" location.

Laurence Leavy is a very successful labor law attorney and a self-made millionaire. In addition to his successful workers' compensation law practice, he owns real estate, a stable of race horses, and has an investment portfolio. He is a baseball and sports fanatic who pays top dollar with his hard-earned money for front row seats. He spent thousands to travel across the country to attend the World Series games in Kansas City, and I found out why he did what he did.

Leavy was shocked when he was diagnosed with liver cancer and told by a doctor that he had only a few more months to live. Fortunately, shortly thereafter he found out that he had been misdiagnosed. Nevertheless, these events changed his life forever. Having faced his mortality, Leavy thought about how he had lived his life. He promised himself that he would have a new, more positive perspective, he would be the best person he could be, and he would live his life to the fullest. Since he was not married and did not have any kids, he decided he would become more philanthropic. With regard to his love of sports, he decided to attend every big sporting event that interested him and spare no cost. One of the pledges he made to himself was to spend whatever amount necessary to get the best seats in the house, every time, for every game he attended. So there he was, sitting right behind home plate at Kauffman Stadium for Games 1 and 2 of the 2014 World Series.

Leavy often runs his law firm of almost forty attorneys and employees from his hotel room using the telephone and the internet, as he travels about 300 days a year from game to game, city to city, sport to sport. In an interview given a few years ago, the Marlins Man says he has attended almost 30 Super Bowls, 90 NBA Finals games, and almost 100 World Series games. Now, everywhere the Marlins Man goes, he is recognized and makes friends along the way. Perhaps he is so well-liked and makes so many friends because he is very generous to others. In fact, each time the Marlins Man attends a game, he gives away several tickets to strangers. All he asks of recipients is just one thing, to "pay it forward."

The Marlin Man's "pay it forward" campaign is simple and life-affirming. In exchange for receiving the free ticket to the game, in one of the best seats in the house, that stranger is asked to do something kind and nice for someone else. He hopes to make the world a better place. Consistent with this theme, while in Kansas City for the World Series, the Marlins Man visited local schools and fire stations to spread the good word.

The Marlins Man has become a true celebrity in the sports world and an ambassador for the game of baseball. He relishes his passion for life, his love for sports, and his noble mission of spreading love and kindness wherever he goes. I feel fortunate to have had the opportunity to meet the man in person at Miller Park in Milwaukee and then again at Arrowhead Stadium in Kansas City. Laurence Levy, may the Baseball Gods always be with you!

Another baseball zealot who has become a great ambassador for the game of baseball is Zack Hample, known to many who follow the game closely as "the ballhawk." For those not familiar with the term, a ballhawk is a person who chases down baseballs at professional ballgames. Hample is the best known ballhawk in the world.

I was introduced to the ballhawk by my son Nate. When Nate graduated from watching sitcoms meant for kids on Nickelodeon, he discovered YouTube. Watching videos on YouTube became one of his favorite hobbies. Since Nate loves videos about baseball, he quickly found ballhawk Hample who became, by far, his favorite YouTuber. I give much of the credit for my son becoming a serious ballhawk to Hample, as well as Nate's increasing obsession with baseball.

I contacted Hample on social media and asked if he would be willing to permit me to interview him for possible inclusion in this book. When he agreed, it felt like another Baseball Gods moment for me and a dream come true for Nate. I told Nate that if it was alright with Hample, he could participate in the interview and prepare questions to ask. Nate could not contain his excitement.

In preparation for the interview, I learned that Hample had written three books about baseball and the art of ballhawking. Who knew that ballhawking was an art? Hample discusses where to position yourself at ballparks and describes his technique for catching baseballs, all based on past experience. He acquires baseballs that are tossed up from players on the field, baseballs that are hit into the stands during batting practice, and home run balls hit into the outfield stands during games. Hample even created a homemade contraption to retrieve balls from difficult places, such as a home run ball that lands in the fountains area at Kauffman Stadium. When it comes teaching fans about ballhawking at ballgames, there is no one better than Zack Hample.

My research revealed that Hample has ballhawked more than 11,000 baseballs and recently celebrated his 1,500th consecutive game catching a baseball at a ballpark. That is truly remarkable. However, Hample may be most famous for catching the 3,000th career hit off of the bat of Alex Rodriguez, a first-inning home run against the Detroit Tigers at Yankee Stadium on Friday, June 19, 2015. This resulted in quite a controversy because Hample initially refused to give this memorable baseball to "A-Rod," but he ultimately did. I actually remember seeing the press conference when Hample graciously presented the ball to A-Rod.

Further research revealed that Hample has caught baseballs in 56 different major league stadiums. He has caught almost 70 home runs during games. Hample's best catch of a home run might actually be the one hit off of the bat of Los Angeles outfielder Mike Trout at Camden Yards on July 24, 2011. It was the first home run of what will almost certainly be a Hall of Fame career. He also caught the 724th home run off of the bat San Francisco Giants outfielder Barry Bonds, who has hit more home runs than anyone. The baseball he considers his all-time favorite is the ball hit by Carlos Beltran on Sunday, September 28, 2008, the last home run ever hit by a Mets player at old Shea Stadium.

Hample has caught more than one home run in a game on multiple occasions. In 2019, he ballhawked 12 baseballs in a single Baltimore Orioles game at Camden Yards. It was the 200th time that he caught more than 10 baseballs at a game. Amazingly, Hample has now caught more than 600 baseballs at Camden Yards. Hample also holds some world records, including one for catching a baseball dropped from 1,050 feet in the air. This ball was dropped from a helicopter.

Nate and I had a list of several subjects to cover during our conference call interview with Hample and a list of questions on each topic. Since I was writing my second baseball book at the time, *The Road to the Show*, we were curious to know if Hample had travelled his own road to the show as a ballplayer. Hample told us that as a kid he always loved baseball. We learned that in his senior year of high school at Columbia Prep in New York City, he went 21 for 29 at the plate, an incredible .724 batting average. While he did not get noticed by major league scouts, he was good enough for college level baseball and played Division 3 at Guilford College. In his freshman year, he went 6 for 14, a solid .429 batting average, but that's when he hit his ceiling.

The Baseball Gods had other plans for Zack Hample. His mother, who always encouraged him to take an interest in scholastics, suggested that he start a journal focusing on things he enjoyed. Since Hample loved baseball, he chose that as his subject. But rather than following his mother's suggestion to start a journal, he wrote a book after his freshman year of college as a summer project. The rest is history. Hample went on to become a true baseball zealot and the greatest ballhawk ever.

Nate and I made sure to ask Hample several questions related to the Baseball Gods, one of my favorite subjects. As a baseball fanatic, Hample was very familiar with the Baseball Gods, but did not believe in them. He was also familiar with the concept of manifesting, but did not manifest or believe in the law of attraction. Hample told us that he was not super-stitious and, in fact, he enjoyed making fun of well-known superstitions, such as it is bad luck to walk under a ladder. Hample said he did not believe in karma, despite his success catching more than 11,000 baseballs, and did not think that the Baseball Gods played any role in his ballhawking success.

The next subject on our list for discussion with Hample was religion. He told us that even though his parents were Jewish, he was not a religious or observant person. Despite having Jewish parents, Hample did not have a Bar Mitzvah when he turned 13, a usual tradition. Hample said that he did not even believe in "good luck" and actually quoted the famous former

Brooklyn Dodgers team owner Branch Rickey with his reply that luck is the residue of design. Hample did agree that some people may be lucky, but added that you can prepare for good luck. He gave an example, the research and preparation he does before each game he ballhawks.

Next, we discussed my thesis that baseball stadiums are cathedrals, and segued from there to another topic important to me, that our body is the real temple. I told Hample that I was a vegetarian tending toward vegan, as was my daughter Kayla and son Nate, and proceeded to ask Hample questions about his eating habits. Zack said that he dated two women in the past that were vegan, but he is not a vegetarian or a vegan. However, he does endorse and strive for a healthy diet. He told us that he started eating salads after college and has never had a Coke, Pepsi, or even a Mountain Dew, perhaps because he was forbidden to drink soda as a kid. He has never smoked cigarettes and has never been drunk. Nate and I were stunned when Hample told us that he has never eaten at McDonald's in his entire life. This adult Hample is in sharp contrast from his days in high school, when he had an unhealthy diet and was called fat by other kids because he weighed over 200 pounds. These days, Hample thinks of himself as a "flexitarian," which he described as a person that is mostly vegetarian but occasionally will eat meat.

Our interview moved to the next topic on our agenda, Hample's charity work. Like Laurence Leavy, the Marlins Man, Hample understands the importance of giving back. He pays it forward by raising money for *Pitch in for Baseball*, a not-for-profit baseball charity that collects baseballs and baseball equipment for underprivileged children around the world.

When Hample caught A-Rod's home run ball, his 3000th hit, the Yankees donated $150,000 to *Pitch in for Baseball* at Hample's request in exchange for the historic baseball. Hample has raised much more than that for his favorite charity over the past several years.

We saved Hample's fascinating career as a ballhawk for our last topic. He told us that his favorite stadium to ballhawk is in Cincinnati, despite giving rave reviews to Camden Yards in Baltimore, Dodgers Stadium in Los Angeles, and Kauffman Stadium in Kansas City. However, his favorite place to ballhawk home run balls is the famous right field porch at Yankee Stadium. That's the spot where baseball legends Babe Ruth, Lou Gehrig and Mickey Mantle planted many a home run. Although Hample is a season ticket holder at Yankee Stadium, he does not have a favorite baseball team. He is proud of his accomplishments as a YouTuber, as an author, as a ballhawk, and as an inspiration to so many kids, like my son Nate, for whom he is the Pied Piper of baseball.

Nate and I really enjoyed our interview with Zack Hample. It was interesting, entertaining and provided quite a bit of new material for my book. As kindred spirits of baseball, we agreed to stay in touch and did so. During his recent visit to Kauffman Stadium, Nate and I got to spend the day with him. Can you guess what the three of us did? We went ballhawking!

To Caitlin, the Stretch Lady, the Cat Suit Guys, the Marlins Man and Zack Hample, may the Baseball Gods always be with you!

CHAPTER THIRTEEN

The Charities

"A life is not important except in the impact it has on other lives."
—Jackie Robinson

LIKE LAURENCE LEAVY, THE MARLINS MAN, AND ZACK Hample, the ballhawk, professional baseball players and their franchises across the nation have been very supportive of charitable causes over the years with their time and money. Almost a century ago, back in the glory days of the New York Yankees, Babe Ruth and Lou Gehrig frequently visited the infirmed in hospitals as they barnstormed across the country. And the important charitable work undertaken in the baseball community today is evident at every level of the game, from the major leagues to grassroot non-profits in small towns throughout the U.S. In my research, I was fascinated to discover that there may well be a direct correlation between baseball teams that were the most charitable and their success on the field.

In 2014, for the first time in thirty years, the Kansas City Royals made it to the American League playoffs. That year, according to statistics compiled by MLB, they ranked behind only the Houston Astros as the most charitable team in baseball as a percentage of payroll. After the Astros and the Royals, the next 8 most charitable teams as a percentage of payroll were the Boston Red Sox, the Arizona Diamondbacks, the New York Mets, the Toronto Blue Jays, the Chicago Cubs, the San Francisco Giants, the Milwaukee Brewers, and the Cincinnati Reds. In 2016, the Boston Red Sox and the Chicago Cubs were ranked as the two most charitable teams in the major leagues, and the Los Angeles Dodgers were right behind them. All 3 teams made it to the playoffs and the Cubs went on the win their first World Series in 108 years. Perhaps the Baseball Gods gave a little boost to teams that were charitably inclined.

When it comes to charitably giving, the Los Angeles Dodgers hit the ball out of the park. The *Adrian and Betsy Gonzalez Foundation* focuses on empowering underprivileged youth in areas of athletics, education and health to better their lives and communities. Adrian Gonzales played first base for the Dodgers for 7 seasons at the end of his career and in 2014 led the National League in runs batted in. Pitcher Clayton Kershaw and his wife Ellen founded *Kershaw's Challenge*, a Christ-centered organization committed to transforming the lives of children in need in the United States and around the globe. Kershaw has won the Cy Young Award as the best pitcher in the National League 3 times, completed the pitcher's "triple crown" in 2011 and was voted the League's MVP in 2014. Kershaw and his wife have been active participants in volunteer work for the last decade and Kershaw, who authored the book *Arise* to raise money for an orphanage in Zambia, has been honored to receive both the Roberto Clemente Award and the Branch Rickey Award in recognition of his humanitarian work. Outfielder Joc Pederson, together with his older brother Champ who has Down Syndrome, raises money for *Best Buddies International*, an organization that helps create opportunities for people with intellectual and developmental disabilities. All-star third baseman Justin Turner and his wife Kourtney created the Justin Turner Foundation, which serves to benefit homeless veterans and children facing life-threatening illnesses. The Foundation hosts an annual charity golf tournament, serves as the official charity of the LA Marathon, and partners with other charities in the LA area to expand its reach. Left-handed starting pitcher Rich Hill partnered with *No Bully*, a non-profit organization with a mission to eradicate bullying and cyberbullying worldwide. Hill visits schools on his anti-bullying campaign to talk to students about building a gentler, more compassionate world for all of us to live in. Kirk Gibson, the Dodgers' 1988 World Series hero, raises money to fight Parkinson's disease through his *Kirk Gibson Foundation*. There are many other examples, but one more in particular to mention, *The Jackie Robinson Foundation*. Founded by Rachel Robinson in 1973 to honor her husband's memory, this organization addresses the achievement gap in higher education by providing college and graduate school scholarships to students of color with limited financial resources. As this demonstrates, Dodger philanthropy goes back decades.

Is it a coincidence that the generosity of the Los Angeles Dodgers may have led to their National League championships in 2017 and 2018? Is a coincidence that in 2017, the year that the Dodgers made it to World Series against the Houston Astros, the team was awarded the Allan H. Selig Award for

Philanthropic Excellence? As for the Astros, in 2017 the team participated in programs to help Houston City schools, rallied support for victims devastated by Hurricane Harvey, and helped transport planeloads of supplies to Puerto Rico after the island was devastated by Hurricane Maria. Charitably speaking, both teams clearly deserved to be there.

I have also seen this correlation between philanthropy off the field and success on the field in my hometown of Kansas City. For example, *Royals Charities*, created in 2001, strives to support children, education, military families, youth baseball and softball in the Kansas City area. It has distributed more than $18 million to many local organizations since its inception. Royals left-fielder Alex Gordon raises money for childhood cancer research through his *Alex's Lemonade Stand Foundation*. Royals pitcher Ian Kennedy frequently serves food at local soup kitchens to help feed the poor and homeless around the Thanksgiving and Christmas holidays. Royals general manager Dayton Moore founded *the "C" You in the Major Leagues Foundation* in January 2014. This organization supports youth baseball, education, faith-based organizations and events, and families in crisis throughout the greater Kansas City area and beyond. Is it a coincidence that the Royals finally made it back to the World Series that year after a 30-year drought?

Even Kansas City's local celebrity baseball fans have found a way to give back to the community. For example, *The Big Slick*, formed in 2010 and now in its tenth year, is the brainchild of actor/comedian and local native Rob Riggle. Every year this organization hosts a Celebrity Weekend of festivities to support Children's Mercy Hospital. These fundraising festivities include a celebrity softball game held at Kauffman Stadium, a charity auction now held at the Sprint Center, a block party, and a bowling tournament. Riggle called upon his friends, Paul Rudd and Jason Sudeikis, fellow actor/comedians and graduates of Shawnee Mission West High School, to help with fundraising activities. Riggle said, "Let's host a poker tournament to raise money for Children's Mercy." All immediately agreed. The poker event was a success raising $122,000 in its first year. Riggle, Rudd, and Sudeikis weren't done. They recruited other well-known actor/comedian friends with roots in Kansas City, including Eric Stonestreet and David Koechner, to become ambassadors of the Celebrity Weekend. *The Big Slick* has blossomed into an important philanthropic undertaking and has now raised more than $12 million for Children's Mercy Hospital, which has become one of the leading pediatric hospitals in the nation.

There is another baseball-related Kansas City charity that deserves recognition and high praise, *Noah's Bandage Project*. The seeds for this organization were planted in 2014 when six-year-old Noah Wilson was diagnosed with a rare form of bone cancer in his spine. Noah underwent treatment and multiple rounds of chemotherapy to address his illness, which included getting poked with needles and having blood drawn for testing almost daily. As a result of these injections and blood draws, his nurses applied Band-Aids to his punctures and wounds. One day, Noah politely asked one of his nurses if she had any Band-Aids other than the boring "brown" Band-Aids he received every day. Maybe some with superheroes on them, he said. The nurse replied that the hospital stocked only the regular, traditional brown ones, but the idea in this young child's mind was percolating.

As the news of Noah's request started to circulate, friends and family from as far away as California started mailing him Band-Aids with lots of colors and designs on them, including some with superheroes on them. As Noah walked up and down the hallways of his hospital, sporting his new colorful Band-Aids, he realized that other kids who were battling serious illnesses would probably like to be wearing happy, colorful Band-Aids too. That is when Noah, and others, decided to expand his idea into a non-profit charity, *Noah's Bandage Project*. With more on his mind than any child of six should have had to deal with as he battled cancer, this amazing little boy had the desire, energy and willpower to help others who were facing similar consequences.

As a distraction from his devasting diagnosis and debilitating treatment, Noah, a die-hard Kansas City Royals fan even at his young age, watched his beloved home team on television every night. And what a magical 2014 season it was for Noah's Royals, which included a wild card playoff game with an epic extra-innings victory and a well-deserved trip to the World Series. In addition to their official and unofficial mascots, Sluggerrr, Redtail and the Cat-Suit Guys, the Royals had another special fan that captured the team's hearts and minds — Noah Wilson.

Noah dreamed of seeing his favorite team in the World Series. The Royals had Noah on their minds and were determined to make this little boy's dream come true. As a result of the Royals season and playoff success, Noah's neighbors started a "GoFundMe" page for the purpose of sending this special kid and his family to the World Series. The page raised so much money, more than $10,000, that the Wilsons were able to buy World Series tickets for other cancer patients and their families in Noah's hospital ward too. On October 22, 2014, Noah attended Game 2 of the 2014 World Series. He cheered as loudly as he could as his favorite team, the Kansas City Royals, defeated the San Francisco Giants 7-2 that night. Noah Wilson got to see his dream come true.

After 14 months of treatment, Noah appeared to have beaten cancer and was declared to be in remission. Shortly thereafter, however, and most unfortunately, a secondary cancer returned and this time Noah did not survive. On June 30, 2015, just seven years old, Noah passed away. After that, *Royals Charities* started collecting boxes of Band-Aids in yellow buckets in Noah's memory. Local Kansas City residents have been helping *Noah's Bandage Project* send out happy packages, filled with colorful Band-Aid's to children all around the country ever since.

Personally, I have volunteered for Noah's charity and it was an unforgettable, rewarding experience. There is nothing like seeing a school gym filled with kids, teenagers, adults and senior citizens, all working together, sorting boxes filled with every different kind of colorful Band-Aid imaginable and then mailing them out to children at hospitals across the nation. With each box that I helped to fill, I knew I was not just sending out colorful Band-Aids. I knew I was sending out love and positive vibrations to individuals, mostly kids, who needed it the most. I also knew that I was helping to continue the idea started years ago by a wonderful, little six-year old boy.

Noah's story is a tragedy, of course, but it is also surprisingly uplifting due to the legacy left behind. Check out the *Noah's Bandage Project* website to learn more about Noah's story and the very wonderful and important work this charitable organization does. Its mission to end childhood cancer through awareness, support and the gift of hope is laudable. The money it raises for pediatric research will save lives. Thank you, Noah Wilson.

As my readers who closely follow baseball will recall, the Kansas City Royals returned to the World Series in 2015 and won the championship for the first time in 30 years. I have a feeling that the Baseball Gods made sure that Noah was with the Royals in spirit as they raised the The Commissioner's Trophy.

Finally, I hope Noah gets another chance at life. Who knows, maybe in his next life he will come back as a professional baseball player. Whatever the future holds, may the Baseball Gods always be with you, Noah Wilson. You are a saint.

CHAPTER FOURTEEN

The Saints

"Are money, fame and power good or bad? The truth is, it depends on how we use it, for example, a knife is neither good or bad. It's determined by who has that knife and how it is used. A thief could use the knife to kill someone to steal what they have. A doctor will use that same knife to save a person's life."

—Radhanath Swami

A SAINT IS AN INDIVIDUAL WHO IS ACKNOWLEDGED AS having an extraordinary degree of holiness. Depending on the religion, saints are recognized either by official declaration, as in the Catholic faith, or by popular acclamation. In Christianity, saints are often depicted with halos as a symbol of holiness. Saints are like earth angels who spread their love and light to make the world a better place. Fortunately, the game of baseball has been blessed with many individuals who are worthy of sainthood.

Pittsburgh Pirate Roberto Clemente, who died in a plane crash while on his way to deliver disaster relief to earthquake victims, was a saint. Brooklyn Dodger Jackie Robinson, who demonstrated love and forgiveness to white racists who berated him, was a saint. Detroit Tiger Hank Greenberg, who dealt with anti-Semitism by hitting home runs instead of punching with his fists, was a saint. New York Yankee Lou Gehrig, with his outstanding integrity and character, was a saint. Los Angeles Dodger Manager Tommy Lasorda, who even in his 90s can be seen around Arizona spring training spreading words of encouragement and inspiration to everyone he meets, is a saint.

Interestingly, as I was researching material for this book, I seemed to find examples of baseball players working their way toward sainthood almost every day. In 2017, outfielder Christian Yelich, playing for the Miami Marlins at the time, got on a plane to attend a "Returning Home" event organized by the *Players Trust* in Dallas, Texas for the benefit of families impacted by natural disasters in California, Florida, Texas, and Puerto Rico. Yelich was joined by more than fifty former and current major league ballplayers who distributed food and supplies to those suffering and most in need. Their presence at the event also helped raise funds for Habitat for Humanity to build and rebuild homes. These players showed their love and light and demonstrated that they were as good with a hammer and nails as they were with baseball bats.

I learned that in December of the same year, former St. Louis Cardinals pitcher Anthony Reyes transitioned from battling Detroit Tiger hitters in the 2006 World Series to fighting wildfires in Los Angeles County. His father was a firefighter and Reyes decided to follow in his footsteps after retiring from baseball. Now, Reyes helps protect the homes and belongings of friends, neighbors and people he hasn't even met, and looks out for Mother Nature's beautiful woodlands as well.

Shortly thereafter, I read that Houston Astros pitcher Lance McCullers was on a quest toward sainthood by helping defenseless animals. After Hurricane Harvey devastated the city of Houston and flooded its streets, McCullers and his wife, Kara, helped to rescue dogs and cats and find new homes for them. Both volunteered to assist "Cloud Nine Rescue Flights" to transport about 150 displaced dogs and cats from Texas to new homes as far away as California.

St. Louis Cardinals catcher Yadier Molina and his wife, Wanda Torres, both born and raised in Puerto Rico, were there to help displaced victims after Hurricane Maria ravaged the island. Through his non-profit organization, "Foundation 4," Molina raised thousands of dollars to assist local residents to rebuild their lives. For these and other humanitarian efforts, Molina was named the recipient of the prestigious Roberto Clemente Award in 2018.

Another saint-like story that must have pleased the Baseball Gods relates to Atlanta Braves pitcher Cole Hamels and his wife Heidi. In 2009, they created The Hamels Foundation, which funds childhood programs in Philadelphia and in Africa. Separately, in 2017, when Hamels was pitching for the Texas Rangers, Cole and Heidi donated their 32,000 square-foot mansion located in southwest Missouri, together with about 100 acres of land, to Camp Barnabas. Barnabas is a Christian charity that operates camps for children with special needs and chronic illnesses. The donation was valued at an estimated $10 million, which I am sure helped the lives of many young kids in need.

As you can see, baseball players may earn baseball sainthood by giving their time, by helping to raise money, or by donating their homes, all in support of important causes. One ballplayer, Seattle Mariner outfielder Braden Bishop, did it differently. He did it with base hits. When Bishop was a kid, his mother Suzy was a successful Emmy Award-winning television producer of shows such as *Jag* and *Law and Order*. Sadly, Suzy was diagnosed with early onset Alzheimer's disease and no longer resembled the person Bishop knew as a child. As a result, Bishop has dedicated his life to educating people about the disease and raising money to fund research to find a cure. His fundraising efforts began while he was a student at the University of Washington. First, he organized a weightlifting competition, "Deadlifts to End Alzheimer's," which raised a few thousand dollars. Then, he decided to start "4MOM," a non-profit charity dedicated to spreading awareness and finding a cure for Alzheimer's. During the 2018 Cactus League season, Bishop expanded his fundraising activities to include baseball. He pledged to donate money for every one of his base hits, $10 for a single, $20 for a double, $30 for a triple, and $40 for every home run. Bishop's pledge went viral and nearly 90 other baseball players joined in, including some pitchers. The pitchers pledged to donate $10 for every batter they struck out and $30 for every batter they walked or hit. It is unfortunate that Bishop's mom Suzy never got to see or understand what her loving son was accomplishing on her behalf. She passed away in October 2019 at the young age of 59.

Whether they are granted true sainthood or not, may the Baseball Gods always be with Christian Yelich, Anthony Reyes, Lance McCullers, Yadier Molina, Cole Hamels, and Braden Bishop.

CHAPTER FIFTEEN

The Sinners

"The Baseball Gods have a way of getting back to people."
—Larry Bowa

THE PREVIOUS CHAPTER CELEBRATES BASEBALL SAINTS.
This chapter chastises baseball sinners. Ballplayers are always
looking for an edge over their opponents. Maybe that is why
"cheating" seems to have been an accepted unwritten rule of
baseball for decades as "a part of the game." Nevertheless,
such actions should not be endorsed or condoned.

Sometimes the cheating is committed by an individual
player, like a pitcher adding a foreign substance to the ball
before he throws a pitch or a hitter adding too much pine tar
to his bat to improve his grip. Sometimes the cheating is done
by management, like a home team heavily watering down
the infield when the other team is known for its speed on the
base paths. However, there can be serious consequences for
these actions. Just go back and reread the chapters on baseball
karma and freak injuries.

Usually, teams cheat to win. But there have been instances where teams actually cheat to purposefully lose. Who could forget the notorious game-fixing scandal in which eight members of the Chicago Black Sox, including the great Shoeless Joe Jackson, were accused of throwing the 1919 World Series against the Cincinnati Reds. The players were paid by gangsters, led by the infamous Arnold Rothstein, to intentionally lose games so sports betting could be rigged in their favor.

This was not the first time this type of sinning at a team level occurred. Back in 1877, the Louisville Grays got busted for cheating and purposefully losing games, just like the Chicago "Black Sox" did four decades later. The Grays' conspiracy was uncovered after the team, then in first place, went on a 1-10 losing streak. Four players who accepted money to lose games were banned from baseball for life and the team went out of business the following season. I suspect this was a case of delayed karma for the teams' sins.

While all sports fans frown upon players and teams that cheat to lose games on purpose, I suspect that some fans might condone, and perhaps even somewhat respect, a player or team that looks for an edge or cheats because they so desperately want to win. For example, Hank Greenberg, the great home-run-hitting first baseman for the Detroit Tigers in the 1930s, admitted in his retirement that the Tigers would find ways to cheat by stealing the opponent's signs to gain a competitive advantage. Greenberg admitted that his chances of hitting a home run increased dramatically if he knew that the next pitch coming was a fastball. (By the way, I suspect this admission might affect Greenberg's candidacy for sainthood.)

The tradition of cheating by stealing an opposing teams'

pitching signs continued into the 1950s and may have played an important role in one of baseball's greatest moments of all time. The New York Giants, my dad's favorite team while he was growing up in the Bronx, cheated using a sophisticated system that included binoculars during the 1951 season. As described more fully in my last baseball book, The *Baseball Gods are Real Vol. 2: The Road to the Show*, the Giants were trailing their hated rivals, the Brooklyn Dodgers, by 13.5 games late in August with little chance of winning the National League pennant. However, the Giants went on a miraculous multi-game winning streak to force a season-ending playoff series. The Giants won the series on a dramatic walk-off home run by Bobby Thomson. Thompson's home run became known as "The Shot Heard Round the World." It certainly was a miraculous Baseball Gods moment, but did Thomson know what pitch was coming before he smashed that ball into the left field seats to win the game? Maybe so, the Giants shortly thereafter lost the 1951 World Series to their other neighborhood rivals, the New York Yankees. Baseball karma at work.

The sin of stealing an opposing pitcher's signs continues to this very day. And with advances in technology, the techniques have become more sophisticated. During the 2018 season, the Boston Red Sox were caught stealing signs in a game against the New York Yankees. Their elaborate scheme involved the sending of electronic communications from the team's video replay room to an athletic trainer in the dugout, using his Apple watch, who relayed the opponents' signs to the Boston players while games were in progress. Apparently, this cheating scheme had been going on for weeks before being discovered. Despites their sins, the Red Sox won 108 games that year and went on to become the World Series champions. Who says life in baseball is always fair?

Perhaps as a consequence of the Red Sox sign stealing scandal, in late 2019 it was revealed that the Houston Astros also sinned their way to success. As first reported by journalists Ken Rosenfeld and Evan Drellich for *The Atlantic* magazine, and later confirmed by an investigation by MLB, the Astros illegally used a sophisticated camera system to steal signs. This bombshell report provided proof that the Astros stole signs during the regular season, during the playoffs that followed, and during the World Series in which they defeated they Dodgers in a terrific 7-game series.

The Astro's methodology included the placement of a camera in the outfield of their home field, Minute Maid Park, focused on the opposing team's catcher. Video footage showing the catcher's sign for the next pitch was transmitted to a staff monitor positioned right next to the Astros' dugout, who would pass the information along to an Astros' player or employee to pass along to the batter. For example, if an off-speed pitch was expected, like a change-up, a trash can would be banged in the dugout. This scandal was uncovered with the assistance of former Astros pitcher Mike Fiers, who blew the whistle on the team. Yet, similar to the Red Sox, the Astros went on to win the 2017 World Series despite their sins.

The buzz around the Houston Astros' quest for an edge over other teams, did not end there. To make matters even worse, die-hard baseball fans accused Jose Altuve of cheating by wearing an electronic device on his right shoulder that buzzed to indicate that an off-speed pitch was coming. I actually recall watching Game 6 of the 2019 American League Championship Series on television when Altuve hit a 2-run walk-off home run against Aroldis Chapman of the New York Yankees to win the game permitting the Astros to advance to the World Series. When Altuve rounded third base and trotted toward home plate, he grabbed his jersey and warned his elated teammates not to tug or remove his uniform. After the game, Fox broadcaster Ken Rosenthal actually asked Altuve about his strange request and Altuve replied with this weak excuse, "I'm too shy. Last time they did that I got in trouble with my wife." I am certain that the Baseball Gods were not pleased with the Astros and consider electronic cheating sins of the highest order. Perhaps that's why they made sure the Astros lost the 2019 World Series to the heavily underdog Washington Nationals. Baseball karma at work.

When it comes to cheating to improve hitting performance, the sins are many. One technique involves "corking a bat." A bat is corked by hollowing it out and filling it with cork or another lighter, less dense substance to make the bat lighter. Arguably, a lighter, corked bat gives a hitter a quicker swing and improves his timing at the plate. Norm Cash, who played almost his entire career with the Detroit Tigers, had 41 home runs and 132 RBI's in 1961, his best year in the major leagues by far and the only year in which he had more than 100 RBIs. After he retired, Cash admitted to *Sports Illustrated* magazine that he used a corked bat during that season and even showed the reporter how he did it. In 1974, during a game against the Detroit Tigers, New York Yankee Graig Nettles, a truly great defensive third baseman, broke his bat on a single and six superballs came flying out of his corked bat. In 1987, during a game against the Chicago Cubs, then Houston Astros player Billy Hatcher broke his bat on a swing and it was discovered that his bat was "corked." Incidentally, 1987 was Hatcher's best year in the majors. Cleveland Indians home run hitting outfielder Albert Belle was caught using a corked bat in 1994. In 1997, Los Angeles Dodgers second baseman Wilton Guerrero, the brother of Vladimir Guerrero, used a corked bat against the St. Louis Cardinals. In 2003, it was discovered that Chicago Cubs home run hitting outfielder Sammy Sosa corked his bat. Finally, in 2020 it was uncovered that Pete Rose used a corked bat while chasing the great Ty Cobb's Major League all-time hits record, which Rose ultimately surpassed.

In baseball, sinning is not limited to batters. Pitchers sin as well. In the 1963 World Series in which Los Angeles Dodgers swept the New York Yankees in four straight games, Yankee pitcher Whitey Ford admitted to throwing "gunk balls." As legend has it, Ford kept a mixture of baby oil, turpentine and rosin in a roll-on dispenser. Ford would also cut baseballs with his wedding ring to "scuff up the ball." If true, these techniques did not help Ford very much. He was the losing pitcher in Games 1 and 4 of that series. Hall of Famer Gaylord Perry, who pitched for a remarkable twenty-two seasons in the major leagues from 1962 through 1983, was famous for throwing "spit balls." Apparently, spitting on the ball alters its movement making it more difficult for a batter to hit. Perry also threw a "puff ball," a pitch that had so much rosin on it that one could see puffs of smoke coming off the ball as it was thrown. Perry also put Vaseline on baseballs to achieve a similar result. Perry was so brazen that even authored a book in 1974, *Me and the Spitter, An Autobiographical Confession,*

in the middle of his outstanding career. In 1987, knuckle-
ball pitcher Joe Niekro was caught using sandpaper on his
finger to scuff up the baseballs. Niekro notched 221 wins in
his Major League career and sandpaper may have played an
important role in that. In Game 3 of the 1988 National League
Championship Series between the Los Angeles Dodgers and
the New York Mets, Dodger pitcher Jay Howell got busted
for putting pine tar in his glove. It didn't help. The Mets won
the game 8-4. In 1999, Detroit Tiger pitcher Brian Moehler
got caught doing a "Niekro." He was nabbed with sandpaper on his thumb while pitching in a game against the Tampa
Bay Devil Rays. In 2004, St. Louis Cardinals manager Tony
La Russa actually admitted to reporters that his pitcher, Julian
Tavarez, hid pine tar under his baseball cap. In 2012, Tampa
Bay Rays pitcher Joel Peralta got nabbed even before the game
started. He was caught with pine tar in his glove during his
pre-game warm-up.

In addition to stealing signs, using electronic surveillance,
corking bats, and spitting on baseballs, there is another very
powerful weapon both pitchers and hitters use to sin to gain
an advantage in the game of baseball — steroids. Performance
enhancing drugs, specifically anabolic steroids, were banned
by MLB in 1991 primarily because of the risk to the personal
health of the players. The second reason they were banned was
because of the unfair advantage it provides to those who take
them. Using steroids is cheating and jeopardizes the honor of
the game.

Anabolic steroids have a dramatic impact on athletes'
strength. As a result, many ballplayers looking for a competitive edge started taking steroids despite the ban and potential

long-term health concerns. The period of time that drug use was running rampant became known as the "steroid era." While this period has no defined beginning or end, it is believed to have started in the late 1980s and continued through the late 2000s. During this period, the number of home runs escalated and long-held home run records began to fall. Steroid use, and the results of the MLB investigation of the steroid era epidemic that followed, put the game's integrity at risk.

Personally, I became convinced that baseball players were taking steroids after Baltimore Orioles outfielder Brady Anderson had a 50-home run season in 1996. This was a dramatic rise from his previous 8 seasons in which he never hit more than 21 home runs. Then, in the years that followed Anderson's incredible 1996 performance, Sammy Sosa and Mark McGwire captured the hearts of America's baseball fans as they battled each other to break the single season home run record. A few years later in 2001, Barry Bonds hit a simply amazing 73 homers, now the single season record, on his way to a total of 762 career home runs, the all-time home run record. It turns out, all of them used steroids.

I assumed at the time, as did many folks who closely followed baseball, that the ball was "juiced," rigged to fly further, or the ballplayers were juiced using steroids. The steroid controversy became a factual certainty when third baseman Ken Caminiti admitted to taking steroids. A year after he retired, Caminiti revealed to *Sports Illustrated* journalist Tom Verducci in 2002 that he started using steroids in 1996 to help him play through an injury. That year, playing for the San Diego Padres, Caminiti won the award as the MVP in the National League. In his confession, Caminiti suggested that perhaps 50% of baseball players were using steroids. I recall at the time feeling validated that what I had assumed to be the case was true, but also feeling sick to my stomach that it was. I felt badly for all the baseball legends whose records had been broken by baseball players who had cheated.

Caminiti may have been the first ballplayer to admit his steroid use, but he wasn't the only one. A few years after the Caminiti bombshell, home run hitter Jose Canseco wrote two books in which he admitted using performance enhancing drugs and called out other players that he suspected also took them. I recall seeing Congressional testimony on TV in 2005 in which Rafael Palmeiro, the Texas Rangers home run hitting first baseman, stated under oath that he did not do and never did steroids. Thereafter, Palmiero tested positive for a steroid called Stanozolol and he could no longer dispute the charge.

As a result of Caminiti's article, Canseco's books, Palmiero's testimony, and concerns about the integrity of the game, MLB started to take the steroid situation more seriously. The league began more regular and rigorous testing and began to issue suspensions for those who tested positive for steroid use. The list of suspended sinners is extensive and includes some of baseball's best including, Alex Rodriquez, Ryan Braun, Miguel Tejada, and Manny Ramirez. Ramirez was even suspended for steroid use twice.

On a somewhat related matter, I recall seeing an interview with legendary Los Angeles Dodger pitcher Sandy Koufax in which he announced his retirement from baseball. Koufax was in the prime of his career at the time, having won 25 or more games in 3 of his last 4 seasons with the lowest ERA in the National League each year. Koufax explained that he needed to get cortisone injections before every game he pitched and he simply did not want to continue getting them. He was concerned that the injections might have a negative impact on his health and body over the long term. He added that he wanted to be able to have a catch with his grandkids someday. The cortisone shots Koufax feared, while legal, were steroids.

I suspect that the Baseball Gods preach forgiveness. Therefore, I am willing to forgive the baseball sinners who cheated during the steroid era for their transgressions. Also, with the passing of time, almost two decades away from that difficult period for baseball fans, I see the steroid issue from a slightly different perspective than I did when I was younger. Now, I can see how the stress of a long season, the desire to compete and win, and the prospects for future monetary rewards might cause a player to break the rules. I still believe, however, that rules are rules and should be followed. I also believe that bad karma and consequences will follow those who choose to break the rules. Just ask any baseball player who would otherwise be in the Hall of Fame, but isn't.

CHAPTER SIXTEEN

The Ghosts

"We are here in Milwaukee. I just saw a ghost. In Ozuna's room,
he saw another one."
—Carlos Martinez

IN MY FIRST BOOK, THE BASEBALL GODS ARE REAL, VOL.
1, I included a quote from Annie Savoy, a character played by
Susan Sarandon in the classic baseball movie *Bull Durham*.
Annie rants about religious disillusionment but admits that
she actually gave religion a chance when she learned that there
were 108 stitches on a baseball and 108 beads on a rosary.
Annie failed to mention that there were also 108 beads on a
mala necklace, which a yogi uses to repeat mantras during
meditation, and that the word "ghost" is written in the Bible
—108 times.

Many books tell tales of the interaction between baseball
and the paranormal world. A primary objective of some of
these authors focused on well-known curses like the "Curse of
the Bambino," which related to the failure of the Boston Red
Sox to win the World Series after trading Babe Ruth to the

New York Yankees, the "Curse of Rocky Colavito," which prevented the Cleveland Indians from winning the World Series after they traded the popular Colavito to the Detroit Tigers, and the "Curse of the Billy Goat," which involved a vindictive fan who in 1945 placed a curse on the Chicago Cubs after being asked to leave Wrigley Field because his goat was bothering other fans. Two of these famous curses have since been broken. The Boston Red Sox won the World Series in 2004 and in 2016, and after exactly 108 years, the Cubs finally won the World Series. The Cleveland Indians still suffer from the Colavito curse but hope to break it sometime soon.

In addition to curses, many of which have been resolved, there is another eerie and unusual paranormal trend in baseball which has not been explained or resolved. This refers to baseball players who claim to have been haunted by ghosts. The first baseball related ghost story I heard occurred in 2011 when Edwin Rodriguez, the manager of the Florida Marlins, now the Miami Marlins, admitted to reporters that he had to console two of his pitchers who were freaked out about ghosts. The Marlins were on a road trip to play the Tampa Bay Rays in St. Petersburg, Florida and were staying at the Vinoy Hotel. After two tough nights hearing strange noises in his hotel room and getting very little sleep, Marlins pitcher Steve Cishek posted on Twitter: "Currently crapping my pants... Can't sleep... My room is def haunted."

Apparently, the Vinoy Hotel, a luxurious and historic Mediterranean-style waterfront hotel built in 1925, already had a reputation as a hotel with a ghost problem dating back many years. Sports writer Gus Garcia-Roberts in his *Miami New Times* article "Florida Marlins Not First Baseball Players

to be Spooked by Ghosts at St. Petersburg's Vinoy Hotel"
quotes Cincinnati Reds reliever Scott Williamson discussing
his scary 2003 experience at the Vinoy:

> I turned the lights out and I saw this faint light com-
> ing from the pool area. And I got this tingling sensation
> going through my body like someone was watching me,
> you know? I was getting a little paranoid. Then I roll
> over to my stomach. And all of the sudden it felt like
> someone was just pushing down, like this pressure, and
> I was having trouble breathing. So I rolled back over. I
> thought 'That's weird.' I did it again, rolled back on my
> stomach. All of sudden, it's like I just couldn't breathe.
> It felt like someone was sitting on me or something. I
> looked, and someone was standing right where the cur-
> tains were. A guy with a coat. And it looked like he was
> from the 40s, or 50s, or 30s – somewhere around that
> era.

Garcia-Roberts' article includes other mysterious Vinoy
ghost-like happenings. For example, pitchers Joey Hamilton
and Billy Koch were spooked by flickering lights, Cito Gaston's
locked and chained door kept opening in the middle of the
night, Jim Fregosi's door suddenly slammed for no apparent
reason, and Brian Roberts and his girlfriend's clothing were
mysteriously moved from the closet to the bed while they were
at the ballpark. According to Garcia-Roberts, Toronto Blue
Jays third base coach Terry Bevington told his players that this
sort of thing always happened at the Vinoy when he managed
the Chicago White Sox. Teammate, pitcher Leo Nunez, must

have already been aware of these ghost tales because he chose to stay at the home of Rays pitcher Joel Peralta, his close friend from the Dominican Republic, rather than at the Vinoy with his team. It seems to me that Marlin's Manager Rodriguez had the right approach to these events. He said, "if the ghost can hit, . . . I'll give him a tryout."

The ghost stories which are alleged to have occurred at the Vinoy Hotel in St. Petersburg could probably be dismissed as ludicrous if it was the only hotel frequented by baseball teams that needed the services of "The Ghostbusters." However, that is not the case. Last year, when I was in Milwaukee on my book tour and met Laurence Leavy, The Marlins Man, at Miller Park, I also made time to visit the notorious Pfister Hotel because I had read so much about its long history of reported ghost sightings, particularly stories related to baseball players. I wrote about this visit, in great detail, in my second baseball publication, *The Baseball Gods are Real Vol. 2 – The Road to the Show.*

Built in 1893, the luxurious Romanesque-revival designed Pfister Hotel, known as the "Grand Hotel of the West," is a member of "Historic Hotels of America," the official program of the National Trust for Historic Preservation. The Pfister is a national treasure and inside the hotel there are more of them. The Pfister has the largest hotel collection of Victorian art in the world. It might also have the largest collection of ghost stories in the world.

According to sports writer Ted Berg's 2013 *USA Today* article "Ghosts Continue Torturing MLB Players at Milwaukee Hotel," apparitions at the Pfister have been taunting and terrorizing hotel guests for at least a decade now. Berg reported that some players, including Pablo Sandoval, refused to stay at the hotel. Sandoval stopped staying at the Pfister ever since he had what he believed to be an encounter with a ghost. Another ballplayer, Mike Cameron, never stayed at the Pfister because of the many ghost stories he previously heard from other players.

In 2018, JR Radcliffe published an article in Milwaukee's *Journal Sentinel* listing the major league ballplayers who claim to have been haunted at the Pfister. The list is impressive, including Adrian Beltre in 2001 who said he heard knocking on his door, Carlos Gomez in 2008 who said everything in the Pfister is scary, Brendan Ryan in 2009 who claimed a light moved through his room, Pablo Sandoval again in 2009 who claimed his iPod started playing music on its own, Michael Young in 2011 who heard footsteps stomping in his room at night, Bryce Harper in 2012 who said his clothing and furniture mysteriously moved in his room, Brandon Phillips in 2013 who reported that the radio in his room turned on by itself, Ji-Man Choi in 2016 who felt the presence of a spirit in his room, and Pedro Alvarez in 2016 who said that his TV went on by itself, not once but twice.

After no reported ghost sightings in 2017, the Pfister Hotel's spooky spirits returned in 2018 with a vengeance when the St. Louis Cardinals were in Milwaukee to play a series against the Brewers. Cardinals pitcher Carlos Martinez reported that one night he could not fall asleep because there was a ghost in his hotel room, a free-floating, full-torso vaporous apparition. Martinez' teammate, outfielder Marcell Ozuna, claimed that he got freaked out too when he saw a ghost in his room. Martinez and Ozuna did not want to be alone for the rest of the night so they packed into a room with Tommy Pham and some Cardinal coaches. Martinez posted all about this ghostly experience in a video on Instagram in which he told his thousands of followers in Spanish that "We are all here. We are all in Peñita's [Francisco Peña's] room. We are all stuck here. We are going to sleep together… If the ghost shows again, we are all going to fight together." I saw it all go down on Instagram and the story went viral in the baseball community.

No doubt, the paranormal experts will continue to debate whether Baseball Ghosts are real or not. Nevertheless, there must be some validity to these unusual, mysterious experiences. Otherwise, why would Travelocity, the well-known online travel site, place the Pfister Hotel tenth on its list of the country's most haunted hotels. Only the Baseball Gods know the answer to that question.

CHAPTER SEVENTEEN

The Walls of Lucca

"And afterward, I will pour out my Spirit on all people. Your sons and
daughters will prophesy, your old men will dream dreams,
your young men will see visions."

—Joel 2:28

ADD KANSAS CITY ROYALS' PLAY-BY-PLAY ANNOUNCER
Steve Physioc to the list of die-hard baseball fans. After forty
years of broadcasting sporting events, how could he not be a
die-hard. Physioc knows all about the Baseball Gods and has
seen countless Baseball Gods moments during his outstanding
career. Over this period of time, Physioc has also seen many
baseball players who have made their dream come true by
making it to the major leagues on their road to "the Show."

Like most ballplayers, sports broadcasters also have to
grind it out for years to make it to their "show," as the voice
of a major league franchise. Physioc began his career after
college with a short stint as Sports Director for KHAS radio
in Hastings, Nebraska, covering local high school and Hastings
College athletics. After improving his professional skills there
through on the job training, Physioc graduated to the college

level and became the WIBW radio voice of the Kansas State Wildcats football and basketball teams in Topeka, Kansas. Physioc made it on his road to the show and began his major league play-by-play announcing career in 1983 when he was hired by the Cincinnati Reds and Cincinnati Bengals. After a four-year run in Ohio, Physioc became an announcer for the San Francisco Giants for two seasons and thereafter joined ESPN for the next several years to call a variety of sporting events, including Major League Baseball, college basketball, and college football.

In the 1990s, Physioc continued to find employment on the West Coast. During this busy decade, he worked as an announcer for San Diego Padres and Pac-10 college football games, for the Golden State Warriors of the NBA, for the Los Angeles Rams of the NFL, and for the Vancouver Grizzlies during their inaugural season. Then in 1996, Physioc was hired by the Anaheim Angels to announce baseball games for their local broadcast and retained that job for the next 13 years.

In November 2009, Physioc was released from the Angels' broadcast crew, along with longtime partner Rex Hudler, ending his 13-year tenure with the franchise. It was the first time Physioc was out of work in his long career. I suspect he realized, as I point out in my book *The Baseball Gods are Real: Vol. 2 – The Road to the Show*, there are always twists and turns and ups and down on the road to the show. Apparently, it is as true for broadcasters as it is for baseball players.

But Physioc was not out of work for long. Knowing that when one door closes, another door opens, he remained patient and kept a positive attitude as he waited for his next job opportunity. In February 2012, Physioc's patience, and his faith in his abilities, was rewarded. Perhaps thanks to the Baseball Gods, Physioc was hired by the Kansas City Royals. Born in Merriam, Kansas, a proverbial stone's throw from Kauffman Stadium, and a graduate of Kansas State University, getting hired to call games on radio and part-time on television for his favorite team since he was a kid was a dream come true. He is now in his tenth season announcing for the Royals franchise.

With more than four decades of experience calling sporting events and ballgames, Physioc could probably write a series of books about sports and baseball. That is why I was not surprised to learn from reading an article on MLB.com that he was already a published author. To my surprise, however, it turns out that Physioc's first publication was not about sports or baseball. His book, *The Walls of Lucca*, was historical fiction about Italy, a family of wine makers, World War I, and the rise of fascism.

Further research revealed that Physioc and his wife, Stacey, went on a trip to Italy in 2006. One night he had the most vivid dream of a city and its inhabitants surrounded by towering walls. The dream was so extraordinary that he was inspired to memorialize his vision on a piece of paper he had close at hand. A few days later, they were traveling to the walled city of Lucca. As they approached in their rental car, and Physioc got his first glimpse, he turned to his wife and said, bewildered, "My gosh, this is it! This is the city that was in my dream!" Jordan Wolf's excellent MLB article, "Royals Voice Physioc Turns Dream into Novel," tells the whole story in detail, and also expands on Physioc's writing philosophy and technique.

Having researched Physioc's extensive broadcasting career and read Wolf's fascinating article about how the idea for his book came to him in a dream, I knew we had a lot in common. We both love baseball, have a spiritual side, and write in our spare time when our primary occupations permit it. And we had something else in common that was truly unusual. Physioc had his dream about a walled city come true and a few years ago I had a past life regression vision about a sunflower field on a farm come true. Not exactly the same, but a coincidence nonetheless.

With so much in common, I decided to mail Physioc a signed copy my first book, *The Baseball Gods are Real – A True Story About Baseball and Spirituality*. I thought if any high-profile baseball personality would appreciate my book about baseball and spirituality, it would be him. What followed was the beginning of a new friendship.

I learned that when *The Baseball Gods are Real* arrived at the Physioc's home, Steve was on a road trip with the Royals. Stacey was the one who received and opened the package, looked at the cover of the book, and turned it over to read the back cover summary. Stacey loved the themes of the book and knew that Steve, who also does yoga, would be excited to read it as well. Stacey took a photo of the book cover and sent it to Steve in a text message.

Physioc was in his hotel room when his mobile phone dinged to notify him that he had just received a text. At the very moment, he was in the midst of writing a chapter for a new fictional book about a Native American boy who grows up to be a baseball player. Just as Physioc was drafting the paragraph to describe his main character pitching in a baseball game, the texted photo of the cover of my book, showing a pitcher squatting on pitcher's mound, popped up on his phone. It was clearly a synchronicity and a Baseball Gods moment.

Steve immediately googled my name, obtained my phone number, and called to thank me for the book. He told me that Stacey was already reading it and racing to finish it because she was certain that he would want to read it as soon as he got home from the road trip. Steve and I talked on the phone for about an hour and, at the end, agreed to meet for lunch when he got back home to Kansas City and settled in.

We met for lunch a few days later, as planned, and Stacey joined us. I took them to one of my favorite restaurants, Zoës Kitchen in Overland Park, the place where my journey to become an author began. We spent our time getting to know one another and discussed synchronicity, yoga, meditation, baseball, my friendship with Jon Perrin, a professional minor league pitcher at the time, and, of course, writing books. We had a great time and it was a pleasure to see what a wonderful, lovely couple they were. They both radiated warmth, love and light.

On the subject of writing, I learned that Physioc's first book was a historical romance inspired by *A Course in Miracles* written by Helen Schucman in 1976. Schucman's book, essentially a self-help book focused on spiritual transformation, gained renewed popularity recently after it was featured on the Oprah Winfrey Show. The author claims that her book was dictated to her, word-for-word, via "inner dictation" from an "inner voice" which she identified as Jesus.

Steve Physioc's *The Walls of Lucca*, is a powerful, very well-written book. It's also a love story filled with emotion and inspiration, with plot twists to engage the reader. When I finished the book, a real page turner, I concluded that Physioc had achieved his goal of telling a very entertaining tale with a very powerful message. In the face of hate and evil, keep God in your heart and practice love and forgiveness. Well done Steve Physioc. May the Baseball Gods always be with you.

CHAPTER EIGHTEEN

The Catcher was a Spy

"I never had it made."
—Jackie Robinson

MORRIS "MOE" BERG WAS BORN TO JEWISH PARENTS ON March 2, 1902 in the Harlem section of New York City just a few blocks from the Polo Grounds Stadium in upper Manhattan. When he was 4 years old, his family moved to Newark, New Jersey and 3 years later, when he was 7, Berg began baseball playing for the Roseville Methodist Episcopal Church team. Since anti-Semitism was widespread at that time in America, the team decided to give him the fake name of "Runt Wolfe," considered a "less Jewish," less ethnic pseud-onym. This may have been the first time that Berg faced adver-sity and alienation because he was Jewish, but it would not be the last.

Berg, as Runt Wolfe, quickly became the church's best player. He went on to become a star at Barrington High School and in his senior year was selected by the *Newark Star Ledger* as a member of the 1918 nine-man "dream team" of the city's best ballplayers. Thereafter, the very bright Berg was admitted to New York University before transferring to Princeton University, where he had a successful college baseball career. Even though Berg was captain of Princeton's baseball team his senior season, his Jewish heritage kept him a social outcast at the university.

Berg did not spend his Friday and Saturday nights at fraternity parties or social activities on campus. Because he was Jewish, he was not welcomed. As a result, he spent almost all his free time at the library. While Berg excelled as a college baseball player on the field, he thrived as an academic in class due to his intelligence and determination. At prestigious Princeton, he learned seven languages, Latin, Greek, French, Spanish, Italian, German, and Sanskrit, and graduated with a B.A. degree, magna cum laude, in modern languages. Mastering these foreign languages would come in handy later in Berg's life. After Princeton, Berg attended Columbia Law School and passed the bar exam.

Berg made his major league debut with the Chicago White Sox in mid-year, having skipped spring training and the first two months of the season to complete his first year of law school. Interestingly, he played his first game as a professional not far from his childhood home, against the New York Yankees, catching pitches thrown to baseball legends Babe Ruth and Lou Gehrig and the other members of the Yankees' famous Murderers Row lineup. Berg would reunite with Ruth and Gehrig years later, when they played together on an all-star team that traveled to Japan for exhibition games.

Considered an average professional ballplayer, Berg's

baseball career was not particularly remarkable. However, he was an excellent defensive catcher and lead the American League in caught-stealing percentage in 1928. He also played 117 consecutive games during his career without making an error, setting a new record at that time. And he was smart. Someone is believed to have said that he was known for being "the brainiest guy in baseball."

Perhaps being an outstanding student at Princeton and Columbia Law, and a 15-year career as a professional baseball player, would be enough for most people. But not for Moe Berg. Berg's next career, as a spy for the United States government, was even more interesting and, as it turned out, much more important.

His espionage activities actually began late in his baseball career in 1934 when he was reunited with Babe Ruth and Lou Gehrig, and other baseball all-stars at that time, to tour Japan to play exhibitions games against the Japanese all-star team. While the rest of the American team was playing a ballgame in Omiya, Berg stayed in Tokyo ostensibly to visit a patient in Saint Luke's Hospital, one of the tallest buildings in the city. Instead, he climbed to the roof of the hospital and used a video camera to film the city and its shipyards. As legend has it, years later the U.S. Air Force used Berg's footage to plan bombing raids over Tokyo in World War II to help win the war.

As a result of Japan's attack on Pearl Harbor years after his retirement from baseball, Berg pursued other ways to do his part for the war effort. First, he accepted a position with Nelson Rockefeller's Office of the Coordination of Inter-American Affairs. A little more than a year later, Berg accepted a position with the Office of Strategic Services,

Special Operations Branch, the unit that developed into the CIA's Special Activities Division. As a member of this branch, Berg took on another mission that was most critical to the war effort against the Nazi regime.

Berg was tasked with determining whether Germany was close to developing a nuclear weapon. He attended a lecture in Zurich and, using his charm, intelligence, and language skills, managed to get to top German nuclear scientist Werner Heisenberg. Based on this interaction, Berg concluded that the Germans did not yet have the bomb, which gave the U.S. and its allies vital information necessary to move forward and defeat Germany.

After the war, President Harry S. Truman awarded Berg the Medal of Freedom for his service, the highest honor given to a civilian during wartime. Without explanation, Berg declined to accept this award. However, after he died, his sister, Ethel, requested and accepted the award on his behalf, which was later donated to the Baseball Hall of Fame.

Two decades after Berg's death, writer Nicholas Dawidoff, a Harvard graduate with a degree in history and literature, magna cum laude, decided to write a biography about Berg. In 1994, he published his first book, *The Catcher Was a Spy: The Mysterious Life of Moe Berg*, which became a best seller. Dawidoff has published several additional books including *The Fly Swatter: A Portrait of an Exceptional Character*, a memoir to his grandfather, which was nominated for the Pulitzer Prize in biography in 2003.

More than two decades after Dawidoff wrote *The Catcher Was a Spy*, Berg's compelling spy story was made into a very entertaining movie with the same title. Paul Rudd in the lead role as Moe Berg gives a truly outstanding performance worthy of an Academy Award. The supporting cast, including award-winning actors Paul Giamatti, Jeff Daniels, and Tom Wilkerson, is outstanding as well. While the film primarily focuses on Berg's life as a spy, it also provides a snapshot of what it was like to be a Jew in America at that time.

In one scene, when Berg was the catcher for the Boston Red Sox, he gets into a taxi cab and the cab driver asks him if he is Moe Berg. Berg replies that he is not, he just looks like him. Clearly, Berg, known to everyone to be a Jew, was uncomfortable admitting who he was. He had been dealing with anti-Semitism and the consequences of his Jewish heritage his entire life. Even though Berg was a proud and patriotic American citizen who fought and risked his life for the United States in World War II, back home, as a Jew, he was still hated by many of his fellow Americans.

It is terribly troublesome to me that, decades later, this kind of anti-Semitism and racism still exists in America today. One unfortunate example recently occurred right in my hometown, on the baseball field, of all places. During the 2019 spring baseball season, I got into a long conversation with a father of one of the other kids on my son Nate's baseball team. He was African-American and his wife Caucasian. His son was new to our team and I saw, from a few practices and games, that the boy was one of the better players on the team, perhaps the best. I asked where his son had played the season before. He replied, on a local recreational team, and proceeded to tell me this story.

As the recreational baseball season grinded on, the father could not help but notice that his very talented son was always positioned in right field and placed last in the batting order. Finally, one day, knowing that his son was a better player than most of the other kids on the team, he approached the coach and said, "Hey, you are always putting my son in the bottom of the batting order and putting him in right field. Any chance you could move him up in the order and try him somewhere else, perhaps at shortstop?" The coach looked the father straight in the eye and said, "No mixed kid is ever going to play shortstop for one of my teams." I was shocked and appalled to hear this tale of bigotry, right here in the seemingly peaceful, polite suburbs of Kansas City, and told him so. The father then said to me, "Oh, c'mon now. That's nothing."

He proceeded to tell me another story that was even more upsetting and nearly broke my heart. Years ago, when he played high school football, he travelled with his team to a small town in western Kansas for a game. He was one of just four black kids on the squad. When they arrived at the football stadium at 10:30am on a Saturday morning, in broad daylight, the field was surrounded by men dressed in all white KKK outfits. Blasting out of a set of speakers on the back of a pick-up truck was "Welcome to the Jungle" a Guns N' Roses song. Sadly, the message was clear. The local police had to be called in to ease and monitor the tense situation. The father told me that he was so irate and offended that he channeled his anger and had a career high for tackles and quarterback sacks that day.

Another very upsetting anti-Semitic incident occurred a few weeks later, much, much closer to home. It indirectly involving my son Nate. Nate and his teammates were in the middle of their pre-game catch when two kids on the team started a conversation which Nate overheard. One kid said, "Hey, you won't believe what happened at my school today. This kid got kicked out of school because he kept yelling out and flashing the "Hail Hitler" sign while walking through the hallways between classes. Then, he was caught drawing Nazi swastikas and Hitler mustaches in the boy's bathroom." The other kid caught the baseball, threw it back, and replied, "That happens in my school all the time." Nate was stunned. As the great-grandchild of Holocaust survivors, he simply could not believe what he heard or that it could have happened. He was irate and offended too.

That evening it was Nate's turn to pitch in the rotation for his team and he had his best pitching performance ever. He must have been channeling his anger, or his inner Sandy Koufax, because he was almost unhittable that night. He completed four innings with only two hits, no walks, and had a career-high of 10 strikeouts.

I simply don't understand bigotry, racism, anti-Semitism, homophobia, or how a person can hate another individual or group just because they have a different skin color or practice another religion. I look forward optimistically to the day when all people realize that we are all humans, we all share one planet, and we are more alike than we are different. That is true regardless of the color of our skin, our religious preferences, where we come from, or what we believe in. Really, we are all the same.

Perhaps Ronald Reagan, our 40th President, said it best during a speech before the United Nations in 1987 in his attempt to unite the countries of world. He said, "Perhaps we need some outside universal threat to make us recognize this common bond. I occasionally think how quickly our differences worldwide would vanish if we were facing an alien threat from outside this world." President Reagan made a compelling point. Faced with a potential global threat, humanity, with all of its different races and religions on planet Earth would quickly unite as one.

CHAPTER NINETEEN

The UFOs

"I will use stories to speak my message and to explain things that have been hidden since the creation of the world."
—Matthew 13:35

IT IS NO SURPRISE THAT RESEARCH SCIENTISTS HAVE HAD a longstanding interest in astronomy and the unknown world of outer space. The U.S. military at the Pentagon, NASA (the National Aeronautics and Space Administration), and the airline industry also have a keen interest in what goes on in the air and above the clouds. You may, however, be surprised to learn that the Vatican shares this interest. In the 1500s, the Vatican built the Gregorian Tower to explore the sky and its stars and the Catholic Church is searching the cosmos still today. The Vatican operates its Advanced Technology Telescope at Mount Graham International Observatory, one of the oldest observatories in the world. This giant telescope is not positioned in Vatican City or even in Italy. It's in Arizona.

Arizona and New Mexico, its neighbor to the east, have had more than their share of conspiracy tales relating to outer space, and possible government cover-ups. One of the most famous of these events is the "Roswell Incident," which occurred in New Mexico in mid-1947 when a "flying disc" crashed at a ranch near the town. The U.S. military claimed that it was just an ordinary weather balloon accident while others came to believe it was an alien spacecraft whose extraterrestrial occupants were captured and detained for research purposes. Even today it is uncertain whether the flying disc was a balloon or an unidentified flying object (UFO). This is the case notwithstanding that ample evidence exists to suggest that Earth has indeed been visited by extraterrestrials. Some of this evidence is of particular interest to me because it is baseball-related. Believe it or not, there have been several claims of UFO sightings at baseball games and ballparks.

The first reported baseball-event, known as "The Mariana Incident," occurred on August 15, 1950 at Legion Stadium in Great Falls, Montana, near Helena. Two UFOs were believed to have been captured on camera before a minor league baseball game. According to reports, the UFOs were sighted by Nick Mariana, the general manager of the Great Falls Electrics, a minor league affiliate of the Brooklyn Dodgers, and Virginia Raunig, his 19-year-old secretary. Mariana and Raunig said they saw "two bright silvery objects rotating and flying at great speed in the sky," which Mariana filmed with his 16 mm movie camera. This tale of the flying saucers was first reported in the *Great Falls Tribune*, the city's local newspaper, the day after it occurred, and later by Maria Saez Perez in an article published with the University of Montana School of Journalism. The event, and Mariana's film footage, was subsequently investigated by the U.S. Air Force. They concluded that what was seen were reflections from two F-94 fighter jets, not UFOs, but one must wonder.

On May 28, 1962, another baseball stadium was visited by a UFO, this time in Vancouver, Canada. This sighting was witnessed by a much larger crowd, including all of the ballplayers on the visiting Portland Beavers and the Vancouver Mounties, the home team, and by the more than 600 baseball fans who were in attendance that night to watch the game. The large, multi-colored object seen by all was described as "a burning satellite," "a comet," "an-off-course rocket," and "a flying saucer." When the story made headline news, it was rebutted by Dr. R. M. Petrie, the Head of the Dominion Astrophysical Observatory in Victoria at the time. He said it was possibly just a meteor or a meteor shower. However, John Lium, a U.S. custom official and a very credible eyewitness who was at the game, disagreed. Lium said, "It was no meteor. It had all the appearance of being powered. It passed overhead at about 400 feet but didn't make a sound." The details of this mysterious event were reported in a ufobc.ca article from the *Flying Saucer Review* entitled "Giant UFO Over Vancouver, Panic at Baseball Match – May 1962." Based on Lium's description, it certainly sounds to me more like a UFO than a meteor.

There is also evidence that could lead a person to believe that seeing a UFO, up close and in person, might have some unexpected, beneficial consequences. Darrell Evans, a 21-year veteran baseball player and 2-time All-Star, was in a terrible batting slump during the 1982 season playing third and sometimes first base for the San Francisco Giants. It appeared at the time that his career was in decline. On one balmy June evening at their home in Pleasanton, California, after a game at Candlestick Park, Evans and his wife, LaDonna, has an extraordinary experience the couple would many months later in 1984 describe to a journalist at the *Miami Herald*:

> One night we were sitting on our porch. It has a great view, into a canyon and we saw something that I'm sure was a UFO. There's no question what it was. It wasn't anything natural. It was about 100 yards away, and 100 or 200 feet up. It was triangle shaped, with a wingspan of about 30 feet. It had a line of red and green lights, and it had a bank of white lights in the back. It didn't make any noise. We thought it might be some kind of experimental craft, because we live near a small airport, but it was midnight, and it didn't come from that direction. And my wife is a stewardess, so she knew it definitely wasn't a plane. It kind of dipped its wings. It was like, 'OK, you see us.' It seemed like it just stopped. It stayed there for 30 seconds.

The Evans' mysterious UFO experience is described in greater detail in Ron Fimrite's excellent 1986 *Sports Illustrated – Vault* article, "A Specialist in Flying Objects."

After his UFO encounter, Evans was reinstated into the Giants' starting lineup, due to a rash of injuries, and broke out of his batting slump. He continued to hit well and had a terrific second half of the season, despite his advanced age, and had a very solid 1983 season as well. As a result of this rejuvenation, Evans signed a new multi-million-dollar contract in the off-season with the Detroit Tigers, who went on to win the 1984 World Series with his help. The next season in 1985, at the age of 38, Evans led the American League in home runs with 40. I'm sure even today Evans and his wife still reminisce about their 1982 UFO experience.

These UFO sightings are by no means limited to North America geographically or to baseball in sports. The reporting of UFO appearances happens globally, at many different types of sporting events, and this has been happening for decades. Perhaps the most incredible UFO sighting occurred in 1954 in Italy at a soccer match in front of a stadium full of 10,000 fans, or should I say witnesses.

On October 27, 1954, professional soccer club Fiorentina, based in Florence, was playing against their rivals Pistoiese in Tuscany at the Stadio Artemi Franchi. During the match, silver, egg-shaped discs traveling at a high speed mysteriously flew into and then hovered over the stadium. As this was happening, the soccer ball rolled to a complete stop, the match came to a sudden halt, and all of the players and fans looked to the sky and pointed their fingers upward. The fans, who probably couldn't believe what they were seeing, started to cheer as they watched the UFOs dance in the sky. For a brief moment in time, players and fans of both teams were united as one, starring at the sky in amazement.

This UFO sighting made headline news across Europe and the British Broadcasting Corporation, now known as BBC, covered the story. In an article written decades later in 2014 by Richard Padula for BBC World Sports entitled "The Day UFOs Stopped Play," Ardico Magnini, who played for Italy during the 1954 World Cup and was on the field that remarkable day in Tuscany, said, "I remember everything from A to

Z. It was something that looked like an egg that was moving slowly, slowly, slowly. Everyone was looking up and also there was some glitter coming down from the sky, silver glitter. We were astonished we had never seen anything like it before. We were absolutely shocked." Gigi Boni, a die-hard Fiorentina fan also in attendance that day, told Padula, "They were moving very fast and then they just stopped. It all lasted a couple of minutes. I would like to describe them as being like Cuban cigars. They just reminded me of Cuban cigars, in the way they looked. I think they were extra-terrestrial. That's what I believe, and there's no other explanation I can give myself."

Incidentally, the season following its UFO experience, Fiorentina went on to win its first league championship ever. Was this a coincidence or did the team's UFO sighting facilitate this beneficial result. Ask Darrell Evans.

Stadio Artemi Franchi stadium in Tuscany was not the only sports venue to witness a UFO sighting. For example, a UFO was spotted at the opening ceremony of the 2012 Summer Olympic Games in London, England. It was at that event that Michael Phelps became the most decorated Olympic athlete of all time, winning his 22nd medal. Also, on May 9, 2015, a UFO was spotted at a professional golf tournament, at The Players Championship at TPC Sawgrass in Ponte Vedra Beach, Florida, southeast of Jacksonville. Rickie Fowler won that tournament defeating Sergio Garcia and Kevin Kisner in a playoff on the final day. And a month later in 2015, thousands of soccer fans in Chile witnessed a UFO when they attended the opening ceremony of Copa America, the main soccer tournament for the national teams in South America. The UFO appeared and for three minutes positioned itself above the stadium before blasting off quickly and disappearing. The shiny, silver flying orb was spotted and captured live on the television broadcast.

According to NUFORC, the National UFO Reporting Center founded in 1974 to catalogue UFO sightings, the number of reported cases is astonishing. From 2001 to 2015 in the United States alone, a stunning 120,000 UFO sightings have been documented, the most in California with the more than 10,000. In America's heartland where I live, Kansas and Missouri residents have reported more than 2,000 UFO sightings. These staggering statistics were revealed to the general public for the first time when the U.S. government finally released its immense files on UFO sightings.

The government continues to disclosure information about UFOs, as well as the possibility of alien life in outer space. In 2017, the U.S. military admitted that they began a secret UFO research program in 2007, which it continued through 2012. Later in the same year, former intelligence officer Luis Elizondo, who lead of the Pentagon research program, told *The Telegraph* "that unidentified flying objects of advanced capabilities have been seen 'lots' over the years." In another interview, he also told *The Independent*, "I think it's pretty clear this is not us, and it's not anyone else, so one has to ask the question where they're from." Officer Elizondo also told reporters that many of the Navy pilots have described experiences seeing aircraft moving and acting in a way that seemed to be beyond current capabilities of the U.S. Air Force.

With a greater focus on the government's release of historical information related to UFOs, it is no surprise that sightings continue unabated and, in fact, seem to be ticking up.

NUFORC reports over 3,700 sightings in 2018, almost 7,000 in 2019, and it expects at least the same amount in 2020.

Interestingly, President Reagan's speech at the U.N. may have been spot on. When UFO's and extraterrestrials visit Earth and hover over our baseball and soccer stadiums, and over the locations of other sporting events, in front of thousands of spectators, could they possibly know which fans in the crowd are Christian, Catholic, Jewish, Muslim, Hindu, Sikh, or Buddhist? Even if they could, would they notice or care? I suspect that all the aliens would see would be human beings living together on this planet.

CHAPTER TWENTY

The American Dream

"Next to religion, baseball has furnished a greater impact on American life than any other institution."
—President Herbert Hoover

WHAT IS "THE AMERICAN DREAM?" HISTORICALLY, IT has a different meaning to different people. Conceptually, its meaning has changed over the years. To Native Americans, even before America got its name, it was the dream of herds of healthy buffalo roaming the plains to provide food throughout the year and clothing to sustain tribes through harsh winters. To the Puritans, the dream was freedom of religion separate from the Church of England and the escape from persecution and possible imprisonment at home. To our forefathers, the dream was rooted in the Declaration of Independence which proclaims that "all men are created equal" with the same "right to life, liberty and the pursuit of happiness." During the periods of the Industrial Revolution and the California Gold Rush, America became the land of opportunity for a better life with the dream of prosperity, success and upward mobility through hard work, discovery and determination. And before and after World Wars I and II, it was the dream of tired, poor, huddled masses of European immigrants sailing into New York Harbor, being welcomed to a new land by the Statue of Liberty.

In more recent times, the concept of the American Dream has found its way into politics. Martin Luther King, Jr. had a dream of an America without racism where every individual had the same civil and economic rights. In its own way, and in this context, baseball has also played an important role in advancing the American Dream. The Dodgers' baseball franchise, whether located in Brooklyn, New York, or in Los Angeles, California, is a perfect example.

My Baseball Gods journey has led me to Dodgers Stadium at Chavez Ravine in LA on three different occasions so far. On each visit, I have made a point to stroll the suite level of the stadium to peruse the interesting display of baseball memorabilia. I am also familiar with Dodger history because I have read two excellent books on this subject. The first, dealt with the 1955 Brooklyn Dodgers, classic underdogs who went on to win their first World Series championship in franchise history by defeating the New York Yankees, the most dominant team in baseball at that time. The second book, focused on pitchers Sandy Koufax and Don Drysdale and how this dominant, dynamic duo led the Los Angeles Dodgers to another World Series championship in 1963, against the same New York Yankees who, incidentally, had won the World Series the previous two seasons.

Every time I walked that suite level, I marveled at the integral part the Dodgers franchise has played in shaping American history. With each step, I saw another legendary collectable documenting each year of the team's significant history. How interesting it would have been to be a fly on the wall during the initial discussions and final decision to sign Jackie Robinson, an African American, to play baseball in, what was at the time, the all-white major leagues.

The signing of Robinson to a major league contract in 1947 by Branch Rickey, the general manager of the Dodgers, had a compelling impact on American society. As the first black ballplayer to make it to "the Show," Robinson, with the help and support of Rickey, paved the way for others to follow. Longer term, it opened a pathway for athletes of color to break barriers in other sports. Most importantly, it gave rise to a greater tolerance towards and understanding of the plight of African-Americans, and ultimately, to all minorities in America. What Martin Luther King Jr. did for his cause with his powerful words, Robinson did, years earlier, with his bat and glove.

In the years that followed the signing of Robinson, the Dodger franchise continued to push the social norms and expand the geographic boundaries of the game. For example, the Dodgers were the first team to sign international players, such as pitcher Fernando Valenzuela from Mexico in 1979, who became the first and only player to win both the National League's Cy Young and Rookie of the Year awards in his first season, and Hideo Nomo from Japan in 1995, who, coincidentally, also won the Rookie of the Year award. This trend continues today, with the rosters of every major league franchise filled with ballplayers born outside of the U.S., most arriving from Central and South America and the Caribbean.

While both baseball and American society, in general, have become much more inclusive in recent decades since the days of Jackie Robinson and Martin Luther King, Jr., there is still a long way to go. America has a dark history that does not get discussed or displayed very often in schools or on television, despite recent events to the contrary. I suspect that for most Americans, it may have been easier to turn a blind eye to it all. Nevertheless, it is extremely important to learn from the mistakes of the past. Therefore, the genocide of Native Americans, slavery, racial segregation, and anti-Semitism that occurred during our nation's short 250-year history, should not be minimized or ignored.

The United States is a great melting pot of people from many countries on planet Earth. Almost, if not all, races, religions and skin colors are represented. I look forward to the day when every person in America has the same opportunity for prosperity, success, and upward mobility for themselves and their children, achieved through good, honest, hard work, in a society that is tolerant and respectful of our individual and religious differences. I also look forward to an America that celebrates all that we have in common and recognizes that we are all the same. Only then will the promise of the American Dream truly be fulfilled.

CHAPTER TWENTY-ONE

The Golden Age

"Never Stop Dreaming."
—Tommy Lasorda

THERE IS A THESIS THAT SAYS: AS GOES THE GAME OF baseball, so goes the United States of America and as goes the United States, so goes the world. It is as if there is a two-way mirror in place and what is happening in the world of baseball at that time is reflected back into our global society, just like the hermetic metaphysical concept of "as above, so below." If this thesis is correct, we should be able to work together to manifest the next "golden age."

As it relates to baseball, many people believe that the first golden age started in the 1920s. The game thrived during this decade, an era known as the "Roaring Twenties," as did the U.S. economy. Business was booming and the economy seemed to grow stronger year after year as new towns and suburbs of existing cities began to pop up all across the country, many with new, bigger baseball stadiums to accommodate the growing, more prosperous population. Decades later, after World War II, the U.S. emerged as a global superpower with the world's strongest military, the most productive and profitable economy, and major league baseball in the U.S., perhaps not coincidently, was the best baseball league in the world.

Some folks believe that the first golden age of baseball actually lasted for a much longer period of time, from the 1920s to the 1960s. Based on my extensive research on the history of the game, I tend to agree. In the 1920s, the focus was on the New York Yankees with Babe Ruth, Lou Gehrig and Murderers' Row. Ruth was the most popular sports figure in America at the time. In the post-depression 1930s, people somehow still found their way to ballparks, perhaps as a way to forget their troubles. The focus was still on the Yankees, but with a different cast of baseball legends, including the great Joe DiMaggio, "The Yankee Clipper." This period also brought the Gashouse Gang to St. Louis, Hank Greenberg to Detroit, and the great Ted Williams to the Boston Red Sox. Jackie Robinson arrived in the 1940s and the face of the game of baseball changed forever. So did DiMaggio's amazing 56-game hitting streak in 1941, a truly astounding record that still stands today. When I think of the golden age of baseball in the 1950s, I see Bobby Thomson hitting a home run "heard around the world," I see the Brooklyn Dodgers and the New York Giants relocating to California and changing the map of baseball, followed by years of expansion. I see Willie Mays, Mickey Mantle, and Duke Snyder roaming centerfields, with young kids throughout America arguing about who of the three was the best. In the 1960s, I see great pitchers Sandy Koufax and Bob Gibson redefine the craft. Koufax may have had the best 5-year pitching streak of the modern era from 1962 through 1966. The fiercely competitive and intimidating Gibson, the best pitcher in baseball from 1965 through 1969, won the Cy Young award and was voted the MVP in the National League in 1968, a year in which he compiled an incredibly low ERA of 1.12, still a modern-day record, and threw 13 shutouts. In Game 1 of the 1968 World Series, Gibson struck out 17 Detroit Tigers to set a new record, breaking the previous record of 15, coincidentally, held by Sandy Koufax.

Conversely, the road baseball has travelled has not always been straight and flat and paved with gold. The road has often faced hills and valleys, some dark periods, and at times considerable controversy. My research for the period from the 1970s through the present revealed, for example, the birth of free agency due to the Curt Flood litigation, which changed the business landscape of baseball forever. That was followed by the creation of a new business, agent representation, which leveled the playing field, so to speak, between ownership and ballplayers. It was an era of Astroturf, multi-purpose football/baseball stadiums with corporate and executive suites, collective bargaining agreements, player labor strikes, large payroll disparities due to lack of a salary cap, a "juiced baseball" conspiracy, stadiums moving in their outfield walls to artificially create more home runs and excitement for fans, franchises selling advertising rights to large corporations who plastered their names on ballpark facades, and scandals using hi-tech techniques to steal signs of opponents. However, the darkest period of all during this period, in my opinion, was "the Steroid Era."

As a result of what turned out to be widespread, long-term use of anabolic steroids by ballplayers to enhance their performance and extend their careers, the integrity of Major League Baseball was put into serious jeopardy. Shock-ridden baseball fans, including die-hard fans like me, became disillusioned with the game. Attendance at the ballparks began to decline. Statistical batting and pitching records, a mainstay for true baseball fans, were called into question. Steroid use had gravely tarnished the great game of baseball and continued reference to it as "America's National Pastime" declined.

I wonder if the MLB lost an entire generation of fans during this period to other sports like football, basketball and soccer, or to other activities available to kids due to technology and the internet. Clearly, baseball faced competition from the growth of video games like Space Invaders, Super Mario, and more recently, Fortnite. Also, nowadays kids spend much more time in front of their personal computers, iPhones, and iPads watching YouTube videos, taking selfies, and scrolling their Facebook accounts and Instagram and Twitter feeds.

Another subtle change has taken place that I believe detracts from the enjoyment of the baseball stadium experience for kids. In 2001, the MLB began a program designed to distinguish officially authenticated baseball memorabilia from fake items on the market. This program is the most comprehensive league-wide memorabilia authentication initiative in professional sports and has become the industry standard for autographed and game-used sports collectibles. The program offers buyers of MLB memorabilia an objective third-party authentication system that guarantees that the item purchased is genuine. This program has merit, especially for collectors, but it tends to reduce the number of baseballs available to young fans because fewer are being tossed to fans in the stands.

Since the best way for a young boy or girl to fall in love with the game of baseball is to walk out of a stadium with a game-used baseball in their hands, and a big, happy smile on his or her face, MLB should reconsider the benefits of this program. I can tell you from personal experience, there is nothing like seeing your son or daughter catch a baseball during a baseball game, hold on to it as if it were gold, and talk about it excitedly for days.

There is another reason why MLB should make every effort to make sure kids learn to love the game of baseball at an early age. It is axiomatic that kids who do will most likely become lifelong loyal fans. Loyal fans turn into paying customers who buy tickets to ballgames. Fans who buy those tickets buy food and drinks at stadium concession counters, and may even purchase a souvenir from the team store. Many will become die-hards, a very beneficial result for the future of baseball.

On the subject of the future of baseball, it may be instructive to revisit the past. Throughout its history, baseball has been extremely resilient. It has survived World War I, the Great Depression, World War II, the Cold War, the terrorist attacks on 9/11, and periods of controversy, including the 'steroid era," which may have been the greatest challenge the sport needed to overcome. As I write the last chapter of this book, baseball, and the entire planet, is facing another very serious challenge, Covid-19, a devil of a virus. Baseball games are being played, but in a shortened season without fans in the stands. Nevertheless, I have every expectation that this great game will continue to find ways to grow, entertain and reinvent itself whenever necessary. Baseball will continue to produce ballplayers with outstanding skills and charisma to thrill their fans for years to come. I suspect, years from now, outfielders like Mike Trout and Mookie Betts and pitchers like Jacob deGrom and Clayton Kershaw will find their way into Baseball's Hall of Fame. There is another "golden age" in baseball's future. Of this, I am certain.

Referring back to the thesis presented at the beginning of this chapter, I also believe that there will be a time in the future when the world and all of its inhabitants will find peace, harmony and prosperity. Achieving this goal begins at the individual level. We must all get back to the basics. Do unto others as you would have them do unto you. Do no harm. Accept your fellow man as he is, with love, kindness and respect, remembering that we are more alike than we are different. Be generous, compassionate, tolerant, humble and kind. Accept, or at least consider, the possibility that a universal, omnipresent higher power may exist, a force, a power far greater than ourselves. When these basic tenets are accepted and mastered by all, we will have opened the gates for all humankind to walk through. We will truly have found the new — Golden Age.

THE CONCLUSION

"You can't make this stuff up. He was definitely
looking over us tonight."
—Mike Trout

IN THIS BOOK, THE BASEBALL GODS ARE REAL: VOLUME 3
- The Religion of Baseball, I properly introduced my readers
to the Baseball Gods. This book investigated the prehistories
of baseball and the religiosity of baseball. I even wrote a chapter celebrating baseball cathedrals. Baseball Gods Volume 3
celebrated the Baseball Gods moments, examples of baseball
players "in the zone," flowing with the holy spirit and showed
reverence for well documented baseball miracles. These pages
also paid homage to the baseball saints, called out the sinners
and celebrated the baseball zealots.

Through the stories in this book, I featured some great
examples of the Baseball Gods at work. I demonstrated to my
readers that baseball karma is real and sometimes it can be
instant and other times it can be delayed and materialize in the
form freak injuries. To avoid freak injuries and bad karma, I
chronical the outrageous rituals and superstitions of baseball

players. I also showed how baseball players and organizations create good karma for themselves with their good deeds and charity work.

In The *Baseball Gods are Real Vol. 3: The Religion of Baseball*, I also explored the mysterious paranormal world of baseball. In these chapters, I investigated baseball ghosts, prophetic dreams and even UFO's! I also showed how baseball is on the front lines of a spiritual war. This supernatural war between the dark and the light reveals itself as a battle between perceived differences over race and religion. While the dark side has successfully used our different races and religions to divide us, the darkness will be on the run when humanity finally realizes that our difference races and religions have more in common than they do differences. I believe that when the American Dream becomes a reality for all American citizens, it will lay the groundwork for the golden age ahead. As goes the game of baseball, so goes the United States of America. As goes the United States of America, so goes the world. One last thing, as you do your part to help bring in the next golden age, may the Baseball Gods be with you!

THE ACKNOWLEDGEMENTS

To Reggie Fink, The Soulmate

To Kayla Fink, The Track & Field Athlete

To Nate Fink, The Ballhawk

To Beth and Jeffrey Fink, The Advisors

To Jonathan Perrin, The Apprentice

To Steve and Stacey Physioc, The Walls of Lucca

To Zack Hample, The Greatest Ballhawk of All Time

To Laurence Leavy, The Marlins Man

To Donna, The Stretch Lady

To John Stoner and Paul Long, The Cat Suit Guys

To Victor Redtail, The Unofficial Mascot

To Paul Rudd, The Catcher was a Spy

To Moe Berg, The American Patriot

To Tim Tebow, The Heisman

To Roberto Clemente, The Humanitarian

To Carlos Martinez and Marcel Ozuna, The Ghostbusters

To Terry Collins and Bruce Bochy, The Managers

To Bubba Derby, The Hero

To Anthony Reyes, The Firefighter

To Drew Blake, The Career Walk Off

To Darrel Evens, The "UFO Watching" MVP

To Steve Scalise, The Whip

To Barry Loudermilk, Jeff Duncan, The Congressman

To Juan Catalan, The Long Shot

To Seman Kuman, The Thai Seal Diver

To Ekapol Chantawons, The Thai Soccer Coach

To Hunt Gillett, The Bat Selection

To Rob Riggle, Paul Rudd, Jason Sudeikis, Eric Stonestreet,
David Koechner, The Big Slick

To Blake Woodruff, The Brother of Brandon Woodruff

To Gretchen Piscotty, The Mother of Stephen Piscotty

To Suzy Bishop, The Television Producer

To Noah Wilson, The Saint

To Jackie Robinson, Shin Soo Choo, Josh Reddick, Jacob deGrom, Noah Syndergaard, David Wright, Yoenis Cespedes, Jeurys Familia, Jason Kipnis, Yan Gomes, Mike Napoli, Lonnie Chisenhall, Chris Gimenez, Cody Decker, Dustin Fowler, James Kaprielian, Jorge Mateo, Sonny Gray, Emmanuel Clase, Alex Avila, Babe Ruth, Johnny Bench, Edinson Volquez, Yordano Ventura, Jose Fernandez, Just Bour, Reymond Fuentes, Alex Gordon, Dee Gordon, Bartolo Colon, Stephen Piscotty, Lou Gehrig, Jose Reyes, Tommy Lasorda, Josias Manzanillo, Keith Hernandez, Manny Ramirez, Jermaine

Dye, Dustin Mohr, Clint Barnes, Chris Coghlan, Kendry Morales, Francisco Liriano, Jeff Kent, Marty Cordova, Rajai Davis, Trevor Bauer, Brian Flynn, Madison Bumgarner, Ned Yost, Martin Perez, Matt Imhof, Mauricio Dubon, Carson Smith, Khris Davis, Blake Snell, Sammy Sosa, Shawn Kelley, Salvador Perez, Carl Crawford, Evan Longoria, Barry Bonds, Roger Clemens, Marc McGuire, Mike Trout, Jose Altuve, Trea Turner, Wilson Ramos, Roger Bernadina, Taylor Jordan, Ian Kennedy, Ian Desmond, Anthony Rendon, Billy Burns, Adam Wainwright, Matt Carpenter, Max Scherzer, Starlin Castro, Joe Maddon, Ben Zobrist, David Bote, Troy Stokes Jr., Mike Lowell, Wade Boggs, Ervin Santana, Yasiel Puig, Turk Wendell, Edwin Encarnacion, Alex Bregman, Moises Alou, Jorge Posada, Ryan Dempster, Ronald Acuna Jr., Tony Watson, Jim Leyland, Tori Hunter, Dayton Moore, Kirk Gibson, Justin Turner, Rich Hill, Alex Rodriguez, Barry Bonds, Jackie Robinson, Clayton Kershaw, Joc Pederson, Hank Greenberg, Christian Yelich, Brandon Bishop, Lance McCullers, Yadier Molina, Cole Hamels, Mitch Haniger, Andrew Moore, Larry Bowa, Shoeless Joe Jackson, Bobby Thompson, Norm Cash, Craig Nettles, Billy Hatcher, Albert Belle, Joe Niekro, Jay Howell, Vladimir Guerrero, Sammy Sosa, Gaylord Perry, Brian Moehler, Tony LaRussa, Julian Tavarez, Joel Peralta, Wilton Guerrero, Whitey Ford, Brady Anderson, Edwin Rodriguez, Steve Cishek, Ken Caminiti, Rafael Palmeiro, Jose Canseco, Sandy Koufax, Scott Williamson, Joey Hamilton, Billy Koch, Cito Gaston, Jim Fregosi, Terry Bevington, Pablo Sandoval, Adrian Beltre, Carlos Gomez, Mike Cameron, Bryce Harper, Brendan Ryan, Michael Young, Brandon Phillips, Ji-Man Choi, Marcell Ozuna, Tommy Phan, Francisco Pena, Don Drysdale, Fernando Valenzuela, Hideo Nomo, Bob Gibson, Mickey Mantle, Joe DiMaggio, Willie Mays, Tommy La Stella, Taylor Cole, Felix Pena, Brad Ausmus, The Baseball Players

JUNE 12, 2019
Jonathan Fink, Zack Hample & Nate Fink
Kauffman Stadium, Kansas City

MAY 1, 2019
Redtail and Jonathan Fink
Kauffman Stadium, Kansas City

JUNE 12, 2019
Zack Hample
Kauffman Stadium, Kansas City

OCTOBER 4, 2019
The Marlins Man
Miller Park, Milwaukee

MAY 9TH, 2019
Nate "10 Strikeouts" Fink and Coach Corey Flynn
Overland Park, KS

APRIL 13, 2019
Coach Corey Flynn's "Good Luck" Coin
Lee Summit, KS

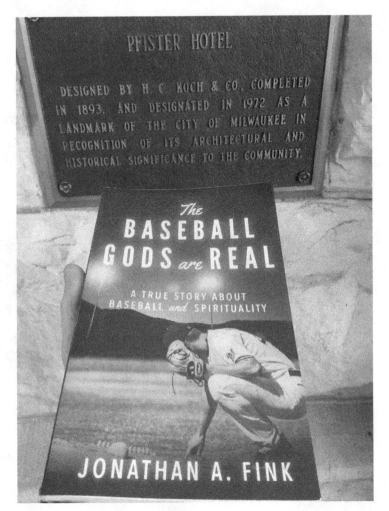

OCTOBER 4, 2018
The Pfister Hotel
Milwaukee, Wisconsin

SEPTEMBER 13, 2018
Steve Physioc, Stacey Physioc & Jonathan Fink
Zoës Kitchen - Overland Park, KS

JUNE 12, 2019
Jonathan and Nate Fink
Kauffman Stadium, Kansas City

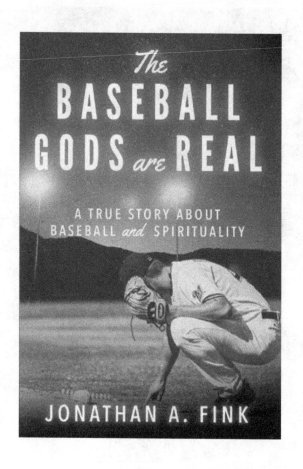

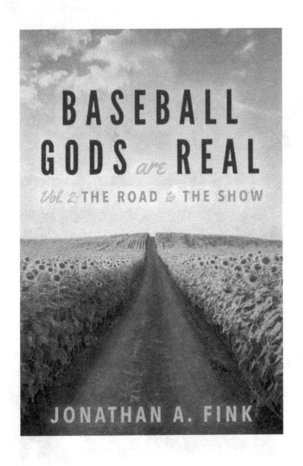